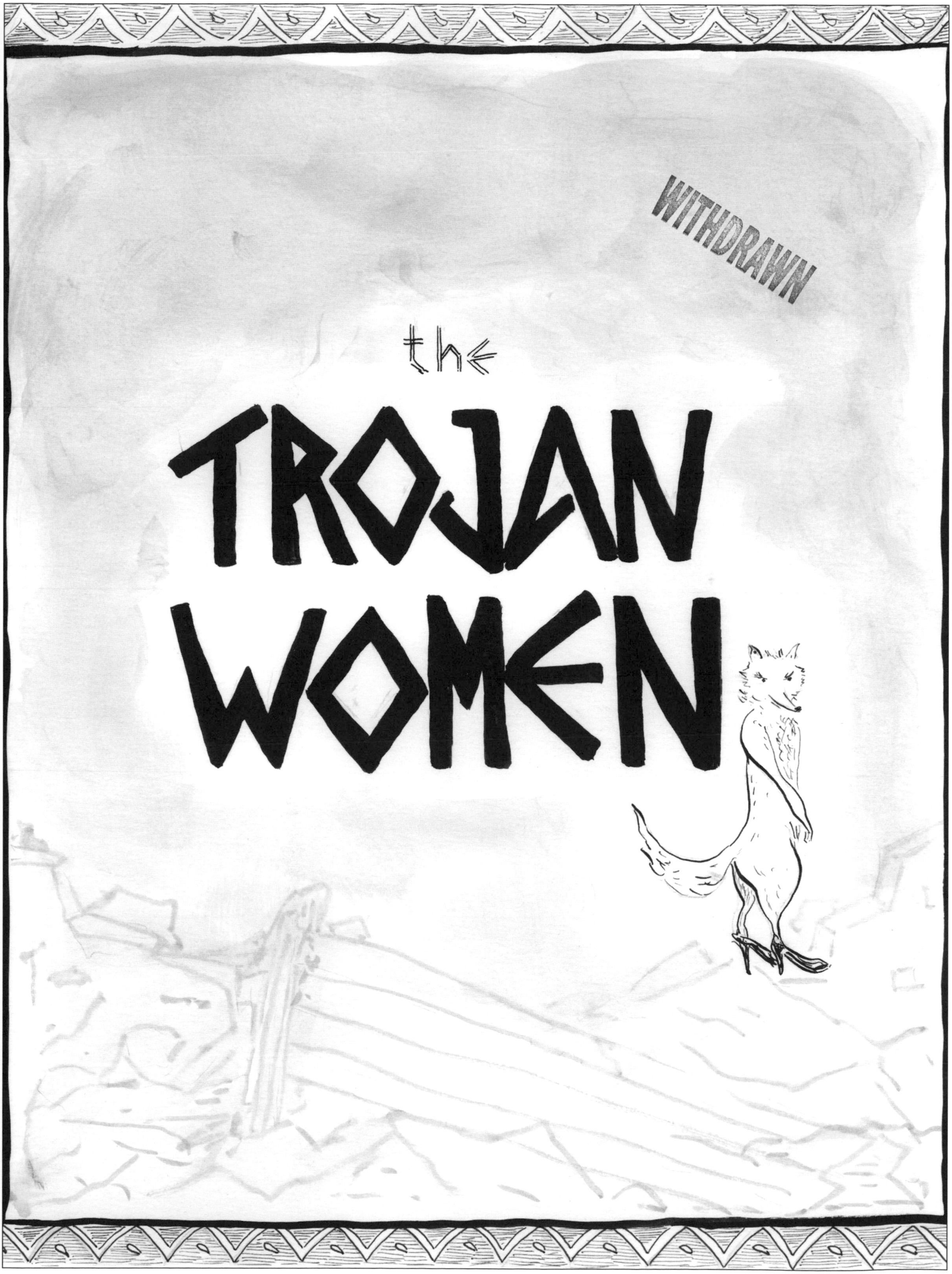
WITHDRAWN
the
TROJAN
WOMEN

EURIPIDES

the

TROJAN WOMEN

A COMIC

by ROSANNA BRUNO

text by ANNE CARSON

A NEW DIRECTIONS BOOK

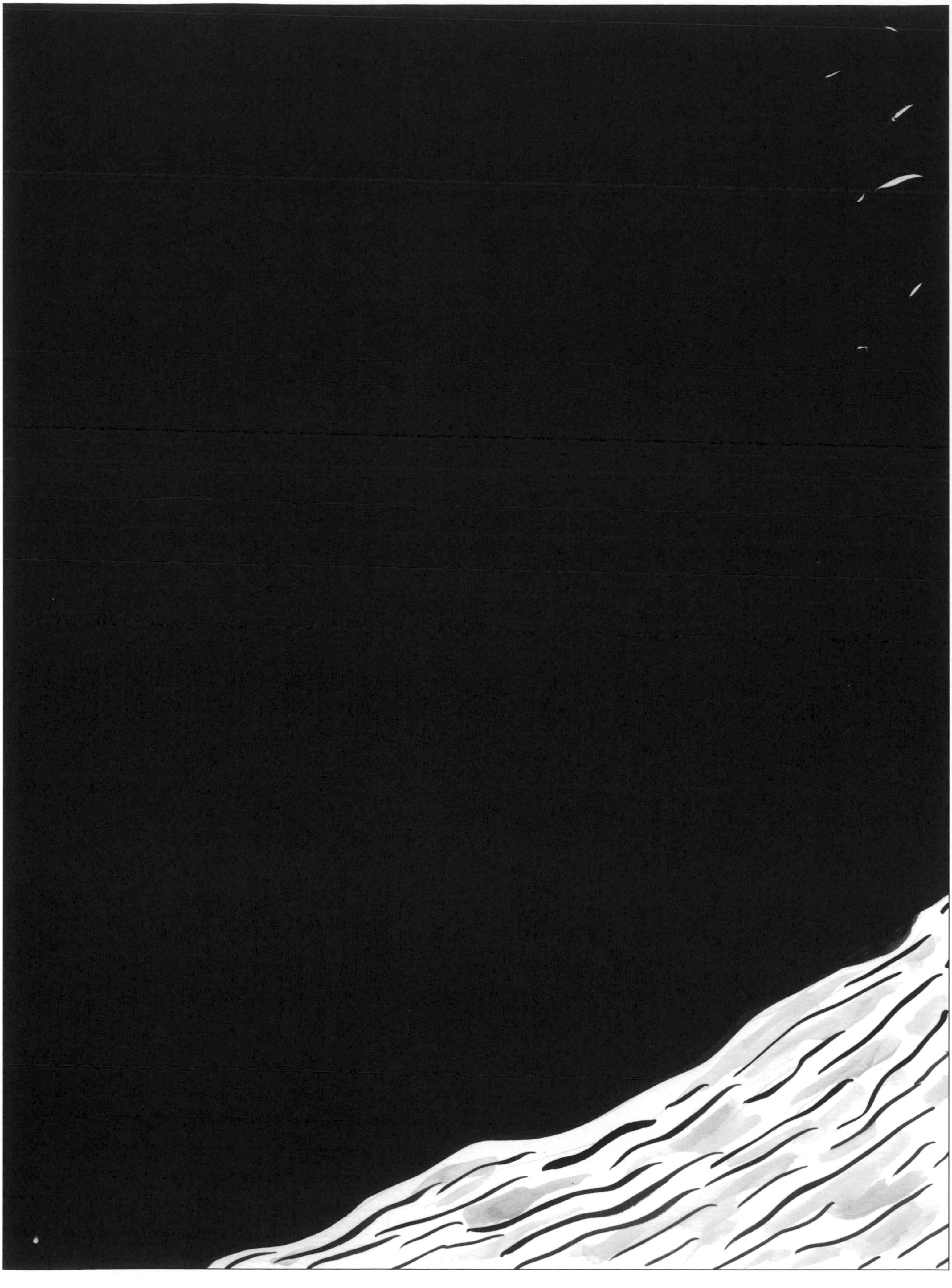

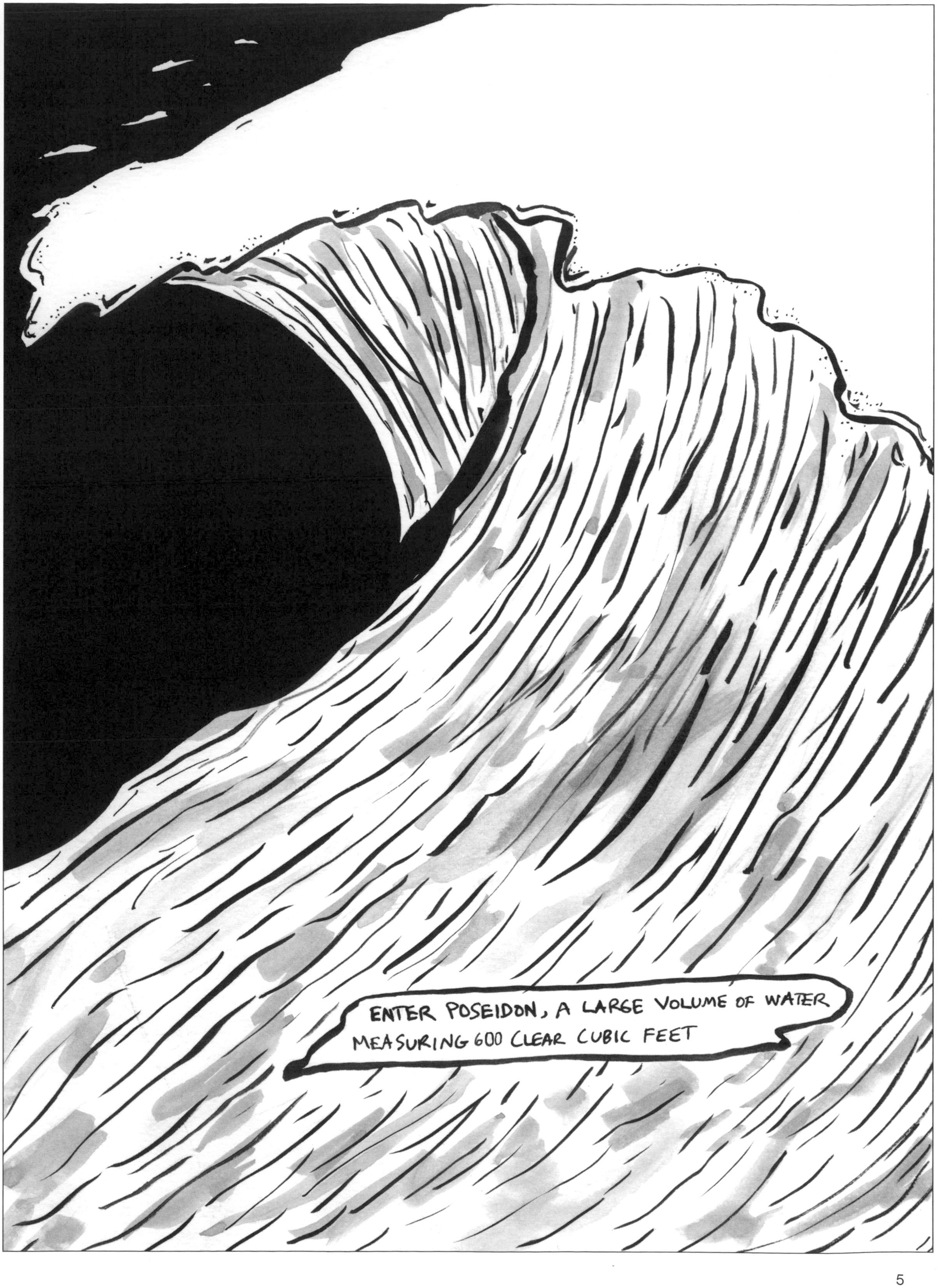
ENTER POSEIDON, A LARGE VOLUME OF WATER MEASURING 600 CLEAR CUBIC FEET

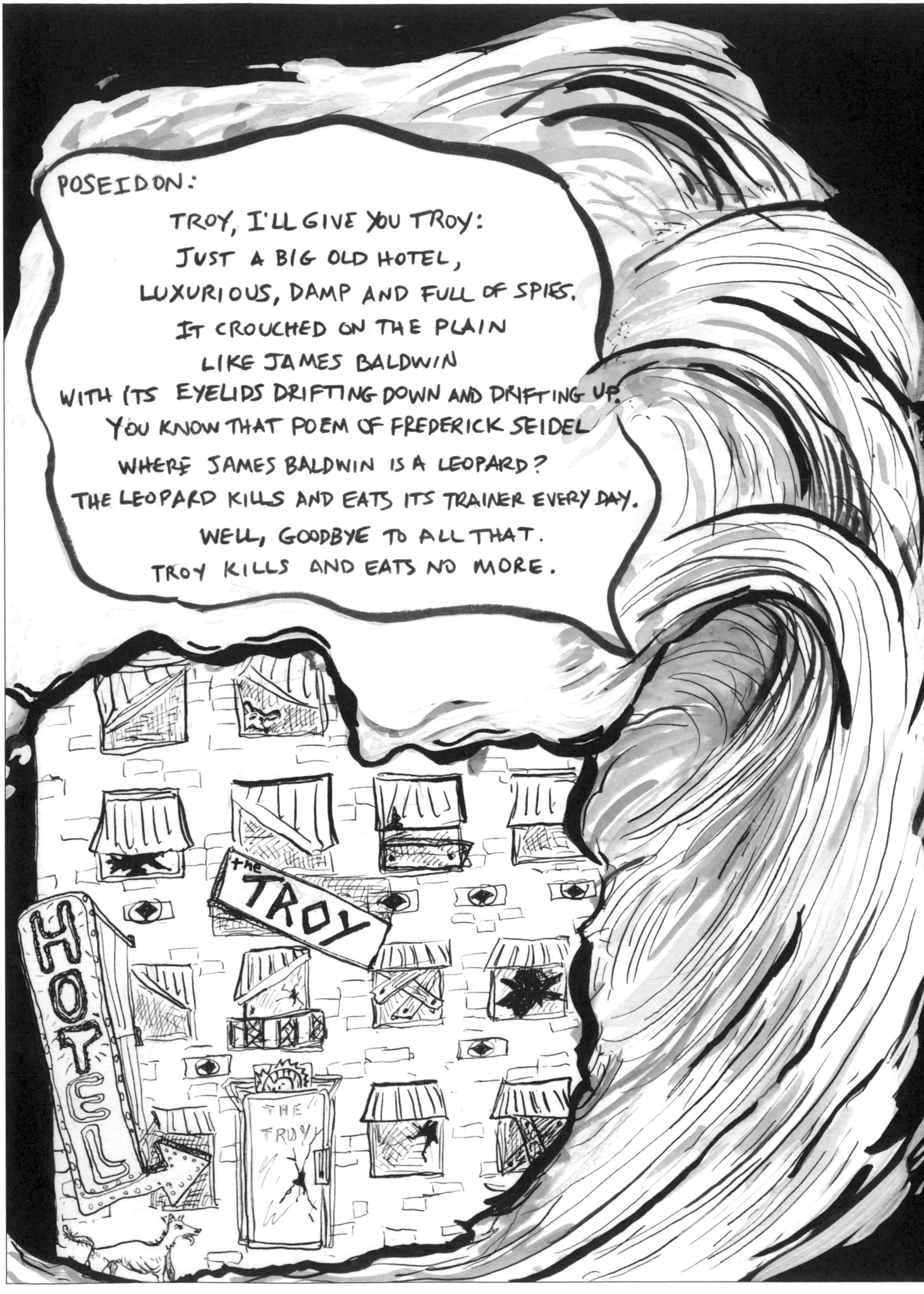
POSEIDON:
TROY, I'LL GIVE YOU TROY:
JUST A BIG OLD HOTEL,
LUXURIOUS, DAMP AND FULL OF SPIES.
IT CROUCHED ON THE PLAIN
LIKE JAMES BALDWIN
WITH ITS EYELIDS DRIFTING DOWN AND DRIFTING UP.
YOU KNOW THAT POEM OF FREDERICK SEIDEL
WHERE JAMES BALDWIN IS A LEOPARD?
THE LEOPARD KILLS AND EATS ITS TRAINER EVERY DAY.
WELL, GOODBYE TO ALL THAT.
TROY KILLS AND EATS NO MORE.
the TROY
HOTEL
THE TROY

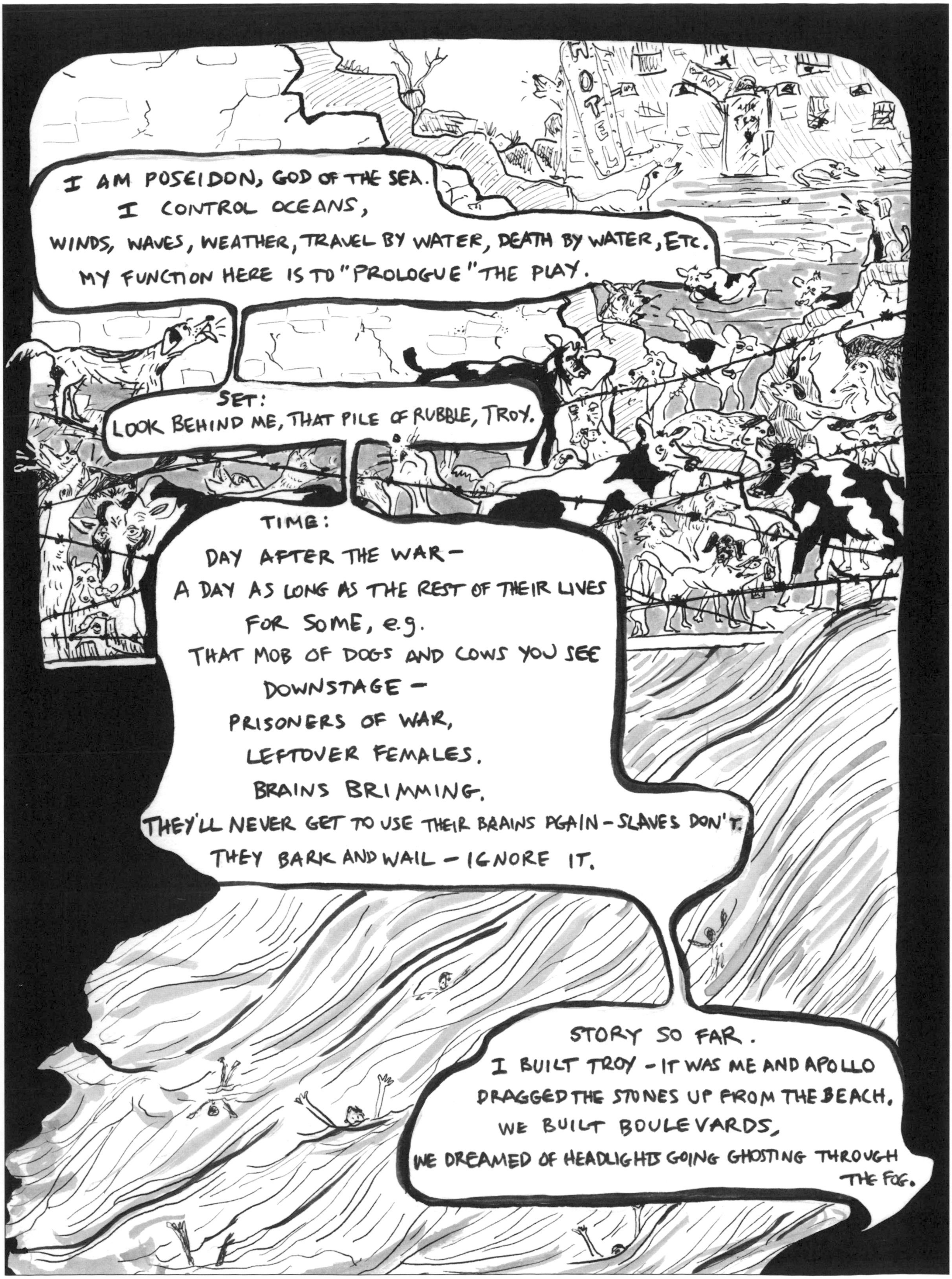
I AM POSEIDON, GOD OF THE SEA.
I CONTROL OCEANS,
WINDS, WAVES, WEATHER, TRAVEL BY WATER, DEATH BY WATER, ETC.
MY FUNCTION HERE IS TO "PROLOGUE" THE PLAY.
SET:
LOOK BEHIND ME, THAT PILE OF RUBBLE, TROY.
TIME:
DAY AFTER THE WAR—
A DAY AS LONG AS THE REST OF THEIR LIVES
FOR SOME, e.g.
THAT MOB OF DOGS AND COWS YOU SEE
DOWNSTAGE—
PRISONERS OF WAR,
LEFTOVER FEMALES.
BRAINS BRIMMING.
THEY'LL NEVER GET TO USE THEIR BRAINS AGAIN—SLAVES DON'T.
THEY BARK AND WAIL—IGNORE IT.
STORY SO FAR.
I BUILT TROY—IT WAS ME AND APOLLO
DRAGGED THE STONES UP FROM THE BEACH,
WE BUILT BOULEVARDS,
WE DREAMED OF HEADLIGHTS GOING GHOSTING THROUGH THE FOG.

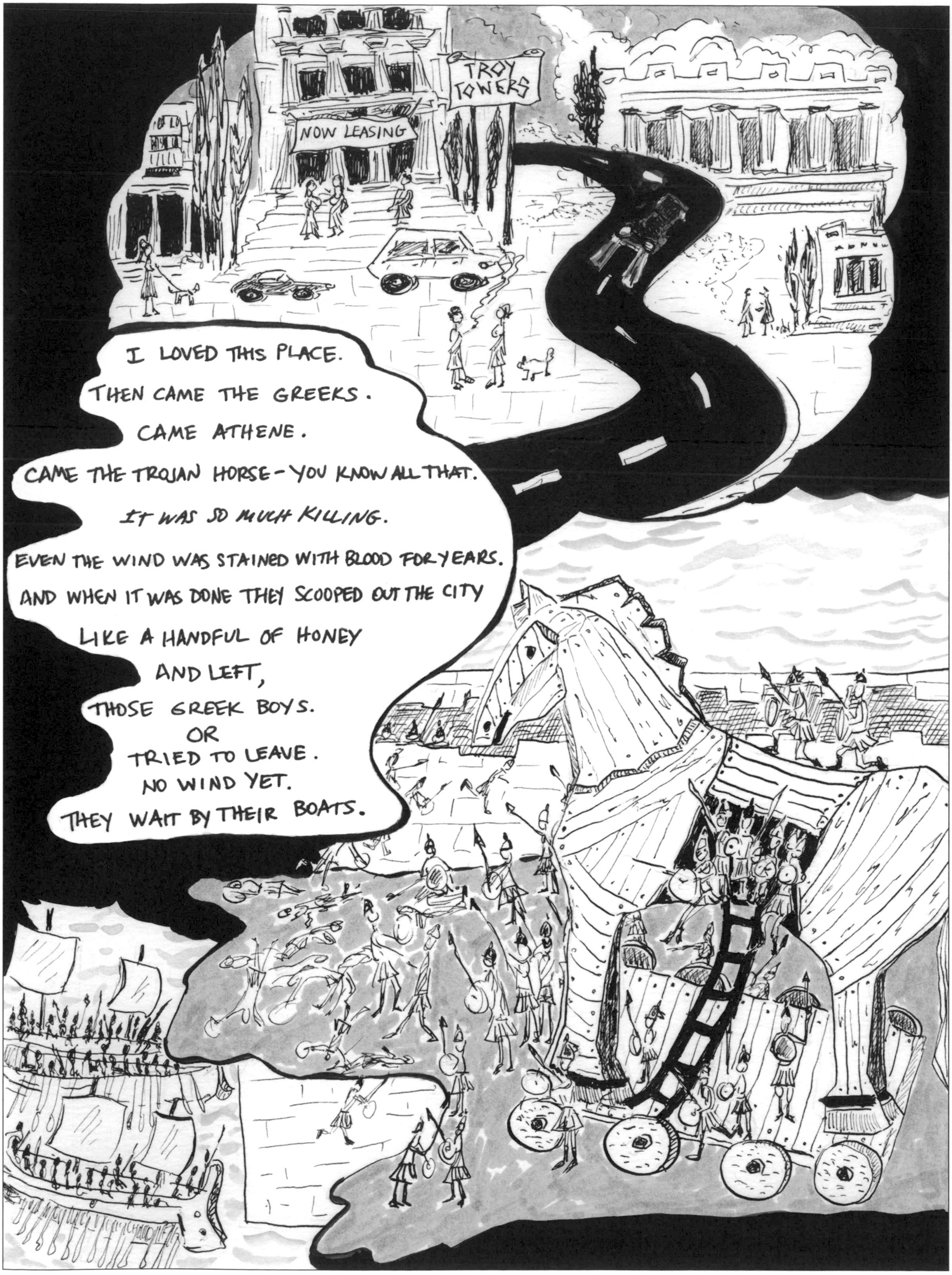
TROY TOWERS
NOW LEASING
I LOVED THIS PLACE.
THEN CAME THE GREEKS.
CAME ATHENE.
CAME THE TROJAN HORSE - YOU KNOW ALL THAT.
IT WAS SO MUCH KILLING.
EVEN THE WIND WAS STAINED WITH BLOOD FOR YEARS.
AND WHEN IT WAS DONE THEY SCOOPED OUT THE CITY
LIKE A HANDFUL OF HONEY
AND LEFT,
THOSE GREEK BOYS.
OR
TRIED TO LEAVE.
NO WIND YET.
THEY WAIT BY THEIR BOATS.

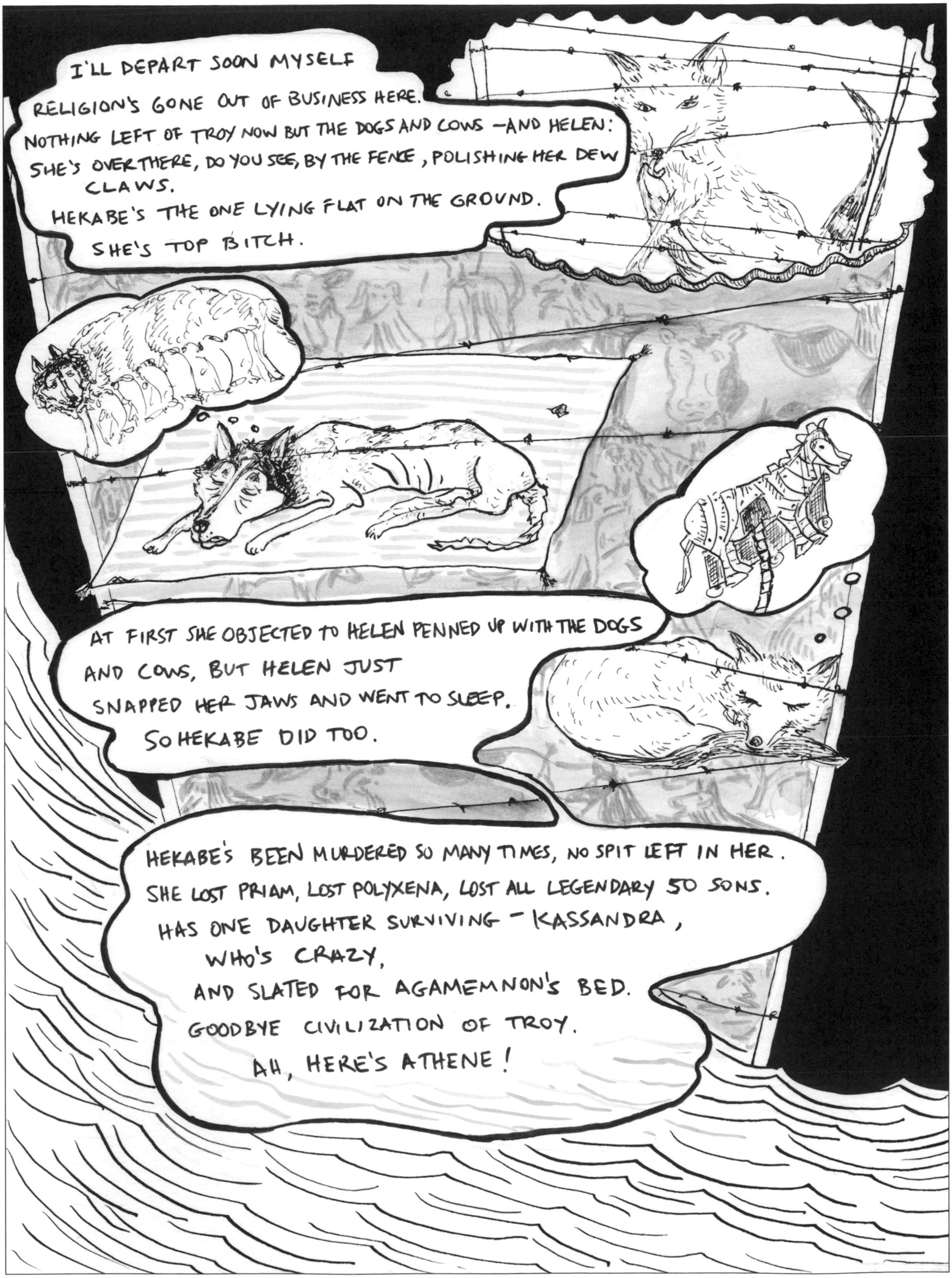
I'LL DEPART SOON MYSELF
RELIGION'S GONE OUT OF BUSINESS HERE.
NOTHING LEFT OF TROY NOW BUT THE DOGS AND COWS —AND HELEN:
SHE'S OVER THERE, DO YOU SEE, BY THE FENCE, POLISHING HER DEW CLAWS.
HEKABE'S THE ONE LYING FLAT ON THE GROUND.
SHE'S TOP BITCH.
AT FIRST SHE OBJECTED TO HELEN PENNED UP WITH THE DOGS AND COWS, BUT HELEN JUST SNAPPED HER JAWS AND WENT TO SLEEP.
SO HEKABE DID TOO.
HEKABE'S BEEN MURDERED SO MANY TIMES, NO SPIT LEFT IN HER.
SHE LOST PRIAM, LOST POLYXENA, LOST ALL LEGENDARY 50 SONS.
HAS ONE DAUGHTER SURVIVING — KASSANDRA, WHO'S CRAZY, AND SLATED FOR AGAMEMNON'S BED.
GOODBYE CIVILIZATION OF TROY.
AH, HERE'S ATHENE!

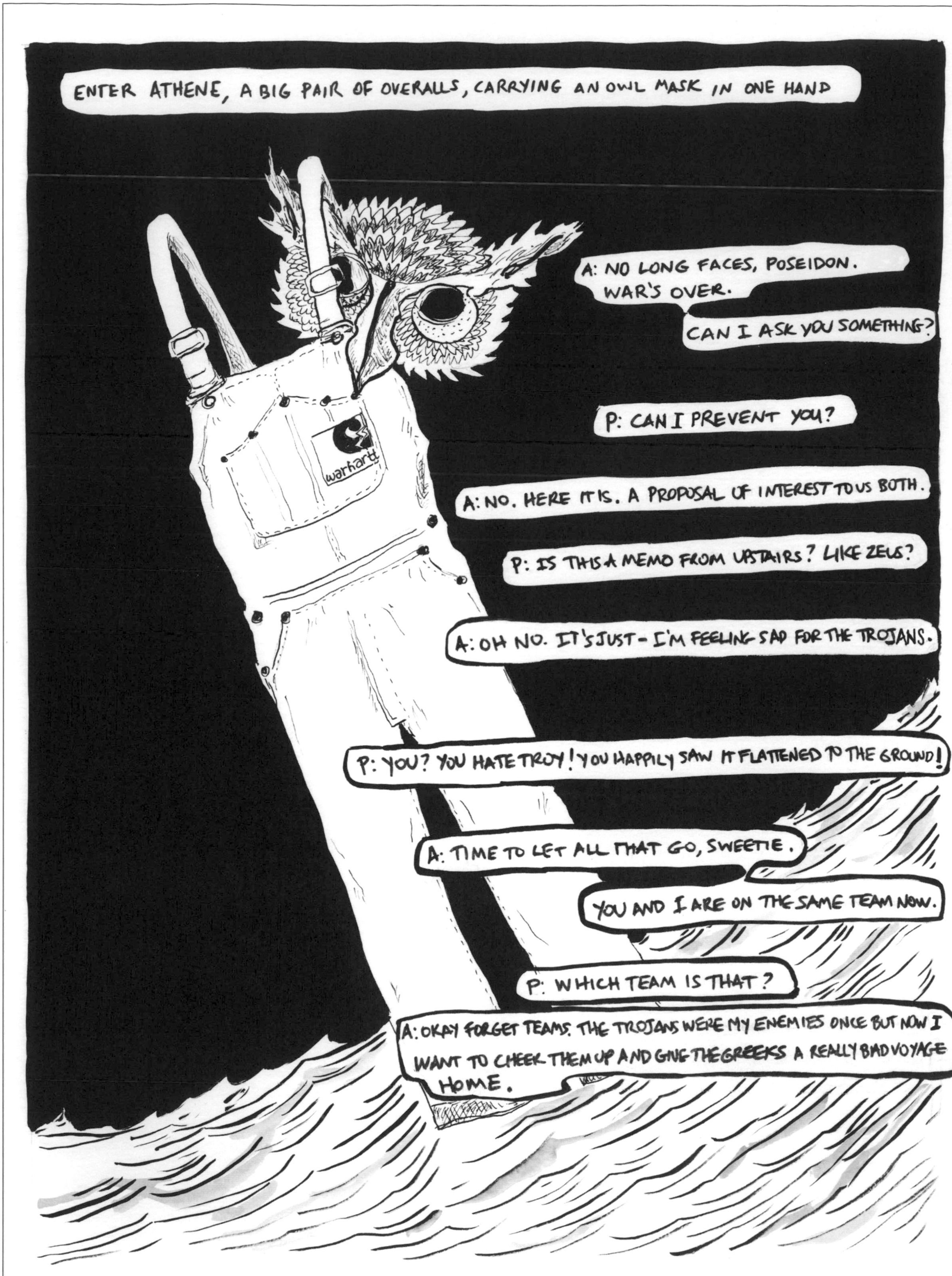
ENTER ATHENE, A BIG PAIR OF OVERALLS, CARRYING AN OWL MASK IN ONE HAND
A: NO LONG FACES, POSEIDON. WAR'S OVER.
CAN I ASK YOU SOMETHING?
P: CAN I PREVENT YOU?
A: NO. HERE IT IS. A PROPOSAL OF INTEREST TO US BOTH.
P: IS THIS A MEMO FROM UPSTAIRS? LIKE ZEUS?
A: OH NO. IT'S JUST - I'M FEELING SAD FOR THE TROJANS.
P: YOU? YOU HATE TROY! YOU HAPPILY SAW IT FLATTENED TO THE GROUND!
A: TIME TO LET ALL THAT GO, SWEETIE.
YOU AND I ARE ON THE SAME TEAM NOW.
P: WHICH TEAM IS THAT?
A: OKAY FORGET TEAMS. THE TROJANS WERE MY ENEMIES ONCE BUT NOW I WANT TO CHEER THEM UP AND GIVE THE GREEKS A REALLY BAD VOYAGE HOME.

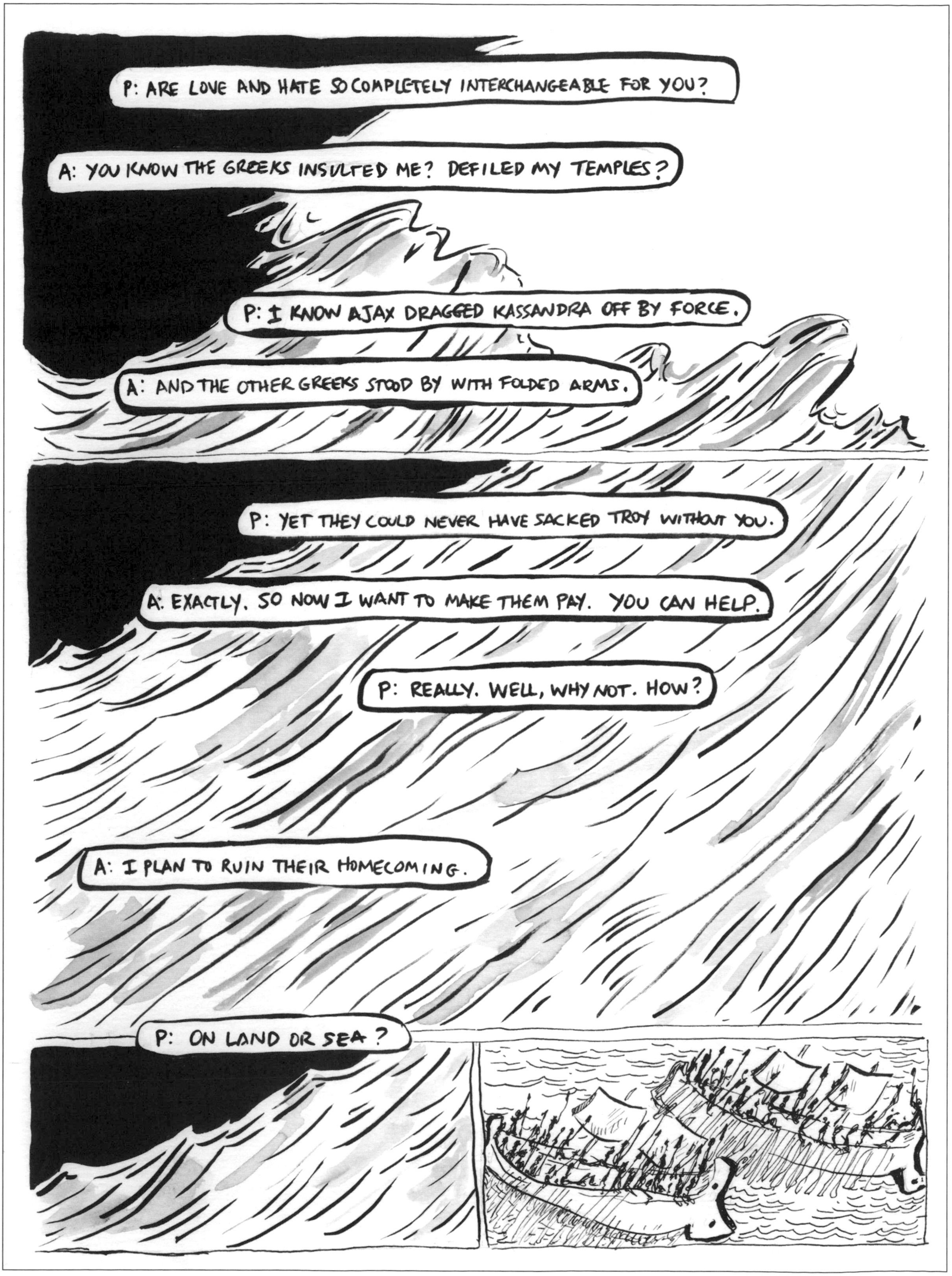
P: ARE LOVE AND HATE SO COMPLETELY INTERCHANGEABLE FOR YOU?
A: YOU KNOW THE GREEKS INSULTED ME? DEFILED MY TEMPLES?
P: I KNOW AJAX DRAGGED KASSANDRA OFF BY FORCE.
A: AND THE OTHER GREEKS STOOD BY WITH FOLDED ARMS.
P: YET THEY COULD NEVER HAVE SACKED TROY WITHOUT YOU.
A: EXACTLY. SO NOW I WANT TO MAKE THEM PAY. YOU CAN HELP.
P: REALLY. WELL, WHY NOT. HOW?
A: I PLAN TO RUIN THEIR HOMECOMING.
P: ON LAND OR SEA?

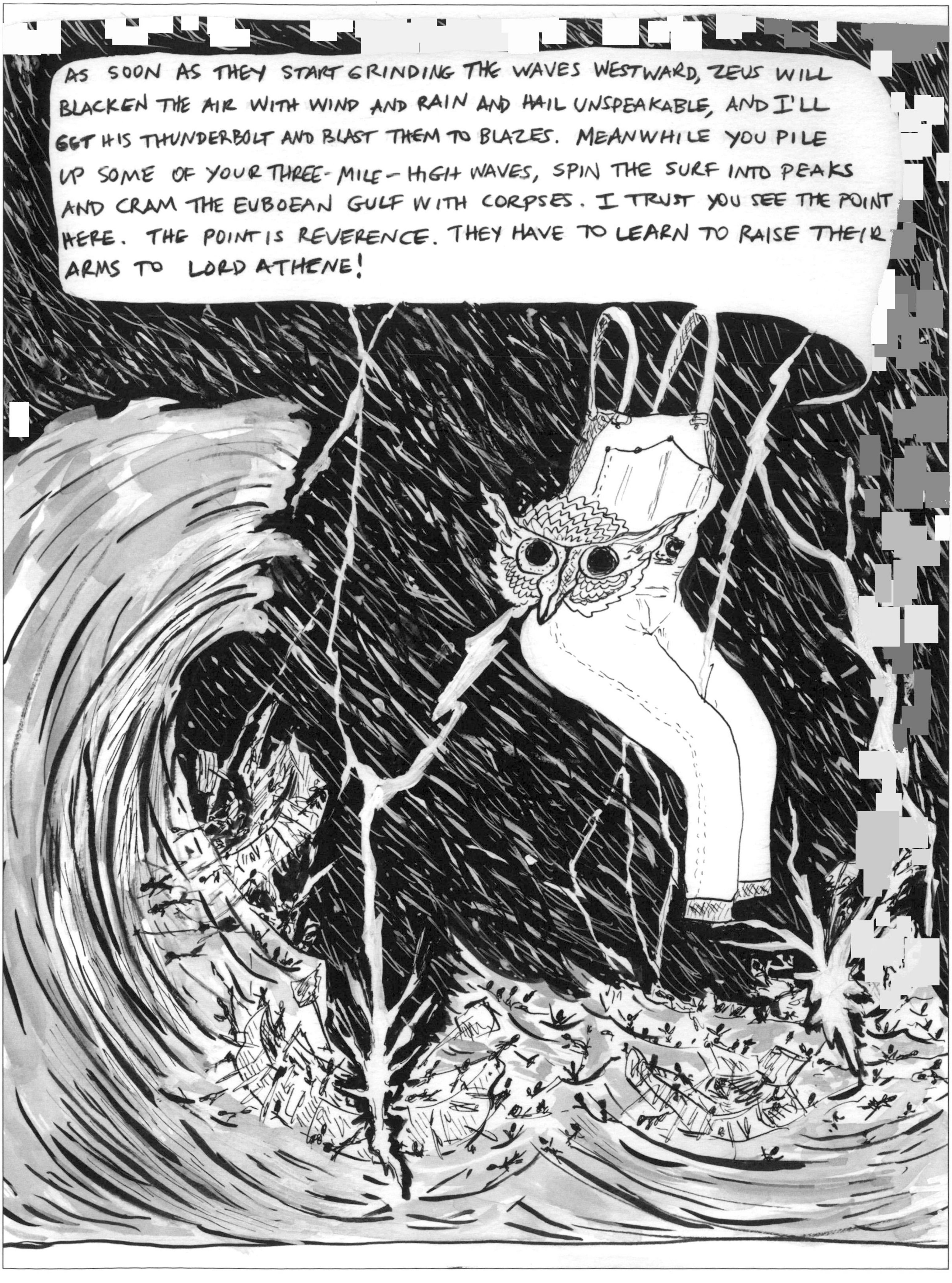
AS SOON AS THEY START GRINDING THE WAVES WESTWARD, ZEUS WILL BLACKEN THE AIR WITH WIND AND RAIN AND HAIL UNSPEAKABLE, AND I'LL GET HIS THUNDERBOLT AND BLAST THEM TO BLAZES. MEANWHILE YOU PILE UP SOME OF YOUR THREE-MILE-HIGH WAVES, SPIN THE SURF INTO PEAKS AND CRAM THE EUBOEAN GULF WITH CORPSES. I TRUST YOU SEE THE POINT HERE. THE POINT IS REVERENCE. THEY HAVE TO LEARN TO RAISE THEIR ARMS TO LORD ATHENE!

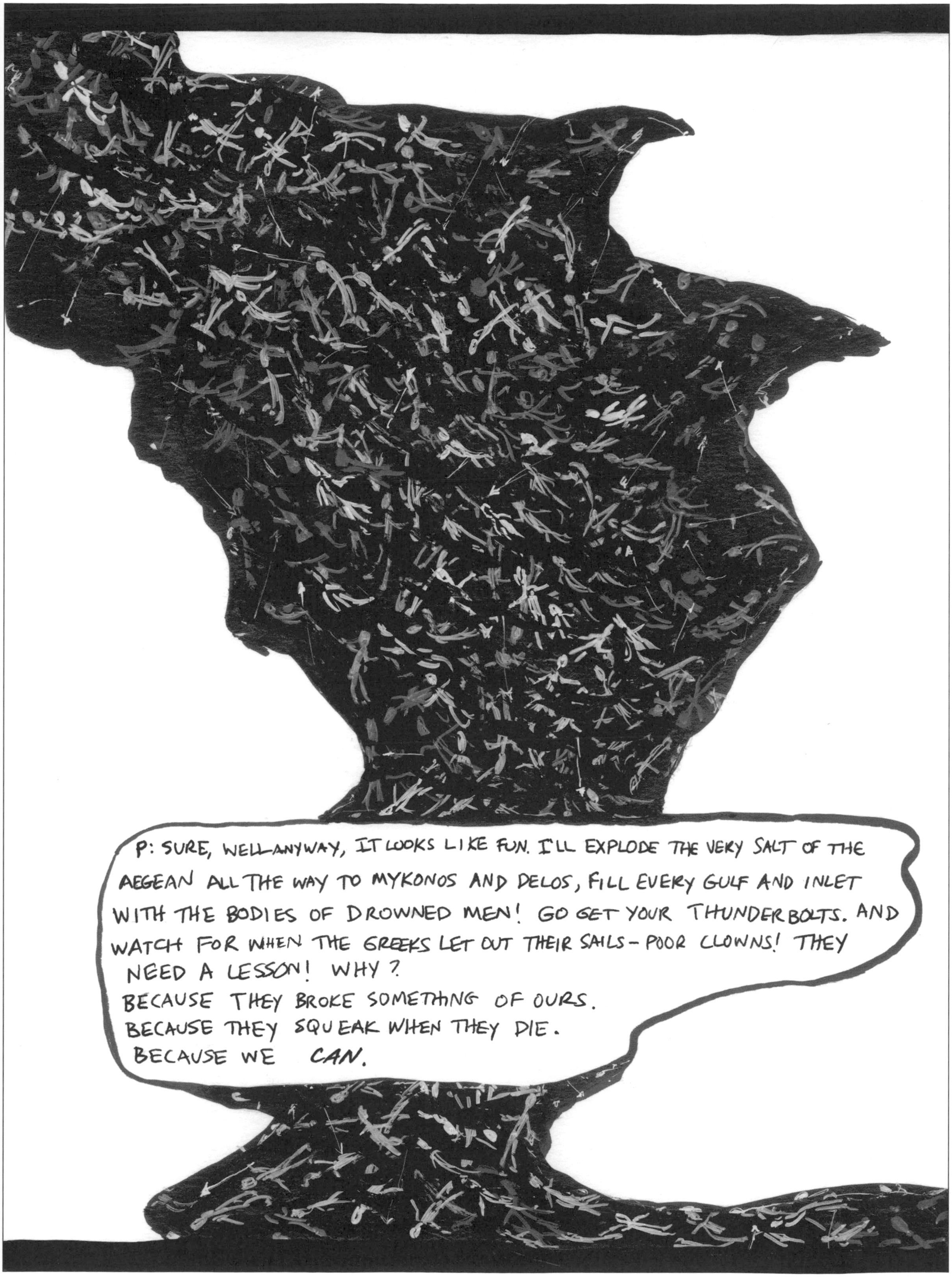
P: SURE, WELL ANYWAY, IT LOOKS LIKE FUN. I'LL EXPLODE THE VERY SALT OF THE AEGEAN ALL THE WAY TO MYKONOS AND DELOS, FILL EVERY GULF AND INLET WITH THE BODIES OF DROWNED MEN! GO GET YOUR THUNDERBOLTS. AND WATCH FOR WHEN THE GREEKS LET OUT THEIR SAILS - POOR CLOWNS! THEY NEED A LESSON! WHY?
BECAUSE THEY BROKE SOMETHING OF OURS.
BECAUSE THEY SQUEAK WHEN THEY DIE.
BECAUSE WE *CAN*.

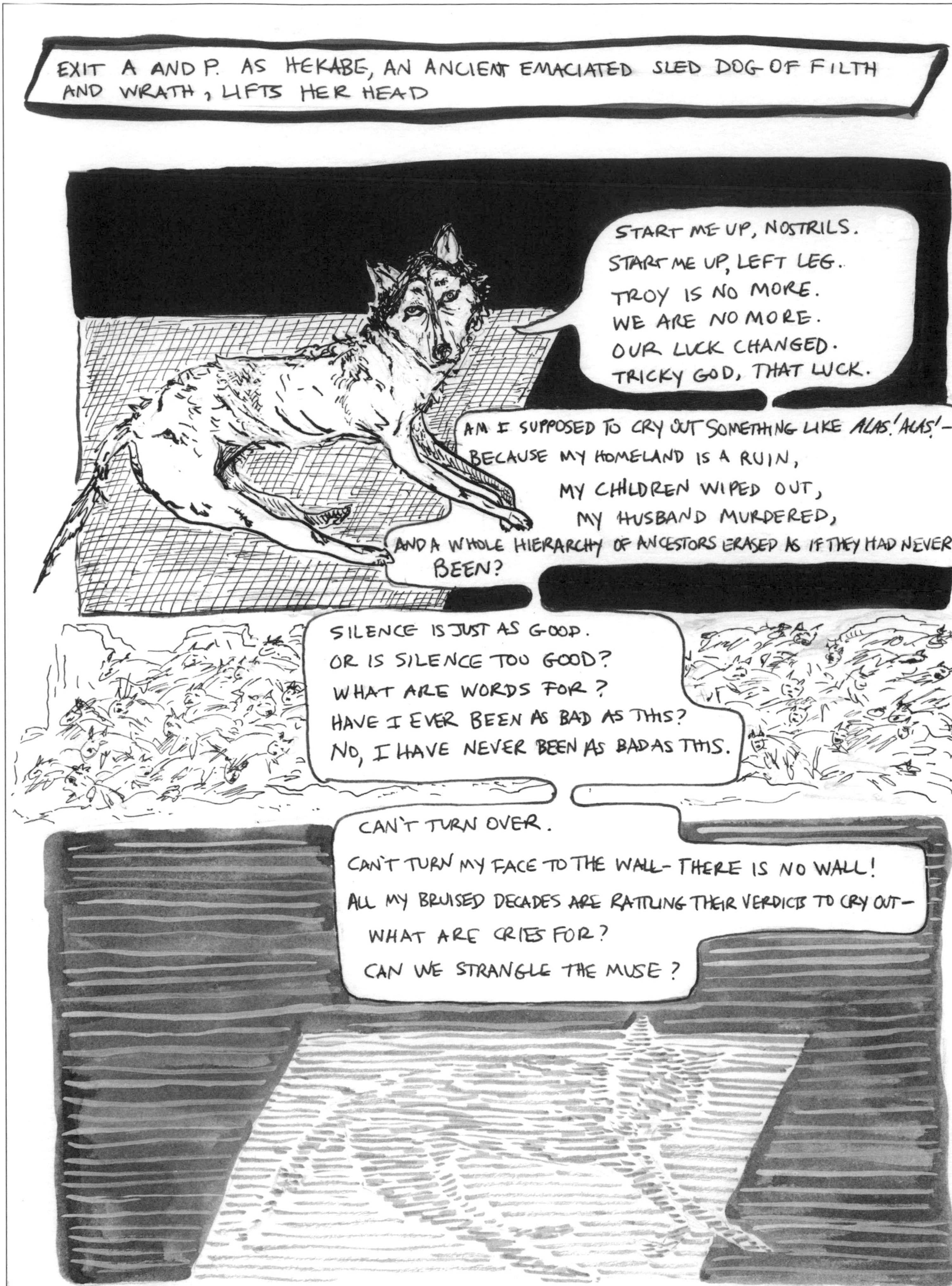
EXIT A AND P. AS HEKABE, AN ANCIENT EMACIATED SLED DOG OF FILTH AND WRATH, LIFTS HER HEAD
START ME UP, NOSTRILS. START ME UP, LEFT LEG. TROY IS NO MORE. WE ARE NO MORE. OUR LUCK CHANGED. TRICKY GOD, THAT LUCK.
AM I SUPPOSED TO CRY OUT SOMETHING LIKE *ALAS! ALAS!*— BECAUSE MY HOMELAND IS A RUIN, MY CHILDREN WIPED OUT, MY HUSBAND MURDERED, AND A WHOLE HIERARCHY OF ANCESTORS ERASED AS IF THEY HAD NEVER BEEN?
SILENCE IS JUST AS GOOD. OR IS SILENCE TOO GOOD? WHAT ARE WORDS FOR? HAVE I EVER BEEN AS BAD AS THIS? NO, I HAVE NEVER BEEN AS BAD AS THIS.
CAN'T TURN OVER. CAN'T TURN MY FACE TO THE WALL—THERE IS NO WALL! ALL MY BRUISED DECADES ARE RATTLING THEIR VERDICTS TO CRY OUT— WHAT ARE CRIES FOR? CAN WE STRANGLE THE MUSE?

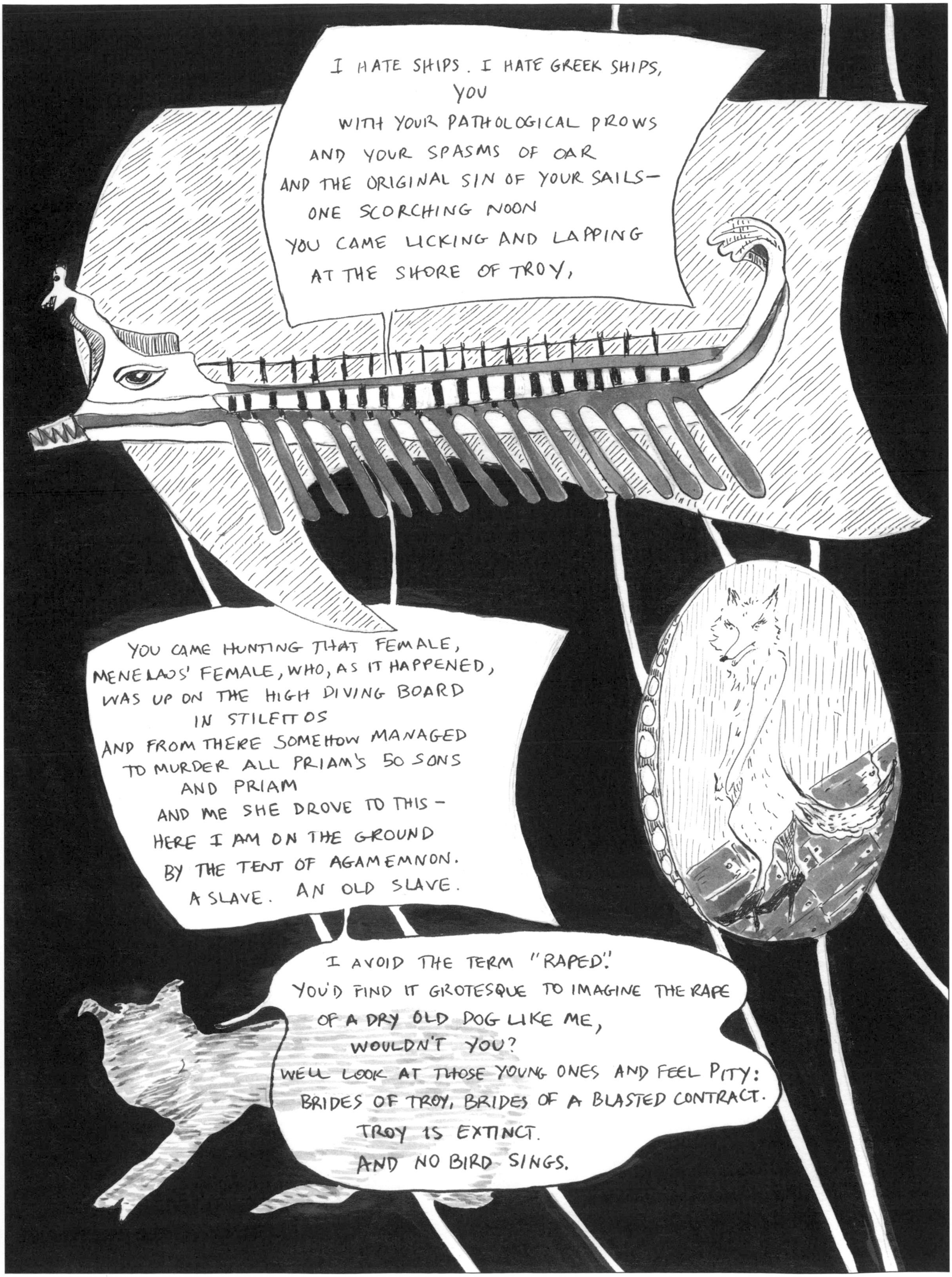
I HATE SHIPS. I HATE GREEK SHIPS,
YOU
WITH YOUR PATHOLOGICAL PROWS
AND YOUR SPASMS OF OAR
AND THE ORIGINAL SIN OF YOUR SAILS—
ONE SCORCHING NOON
YOU CAME LICKING AND LAPPING
AT THE SHORE OF TROY,
YOU CAME HUNTING THAT FEMALE,
MENELAOS' FEMALE, WHO, AS IT HAPPENED,
WAS UP ON THE HIGH DIVING BOARD
IN STILETTOS
AND FROM THERE SOMEHOW MANAGED
TO MURDER ALL PRIAM'S 50 SONS
AND PRIAM
AND ME SHE DROVE TO THIS—
HERE I AM ON THE GROUND
BY THE TENT OF AGAMEMNON.
A SLAVE. AN OLD SLAVE.
I AVOID THE TERM "RAPED."
YOU'D FIND IT GROTESQUE TO IMAGINE THE RAPE
OF A DRY OLD DOG LIKE ME,
WOULDN'T YOU?
WELL LOOK AT THOSE YOUNG ONES AND FEEL PITY:
BRIDES OF TROY, BRIDES OF A BLASTED CONTRACT.
TROY IS EXTINCT.
AND NO BIRD SINGS.

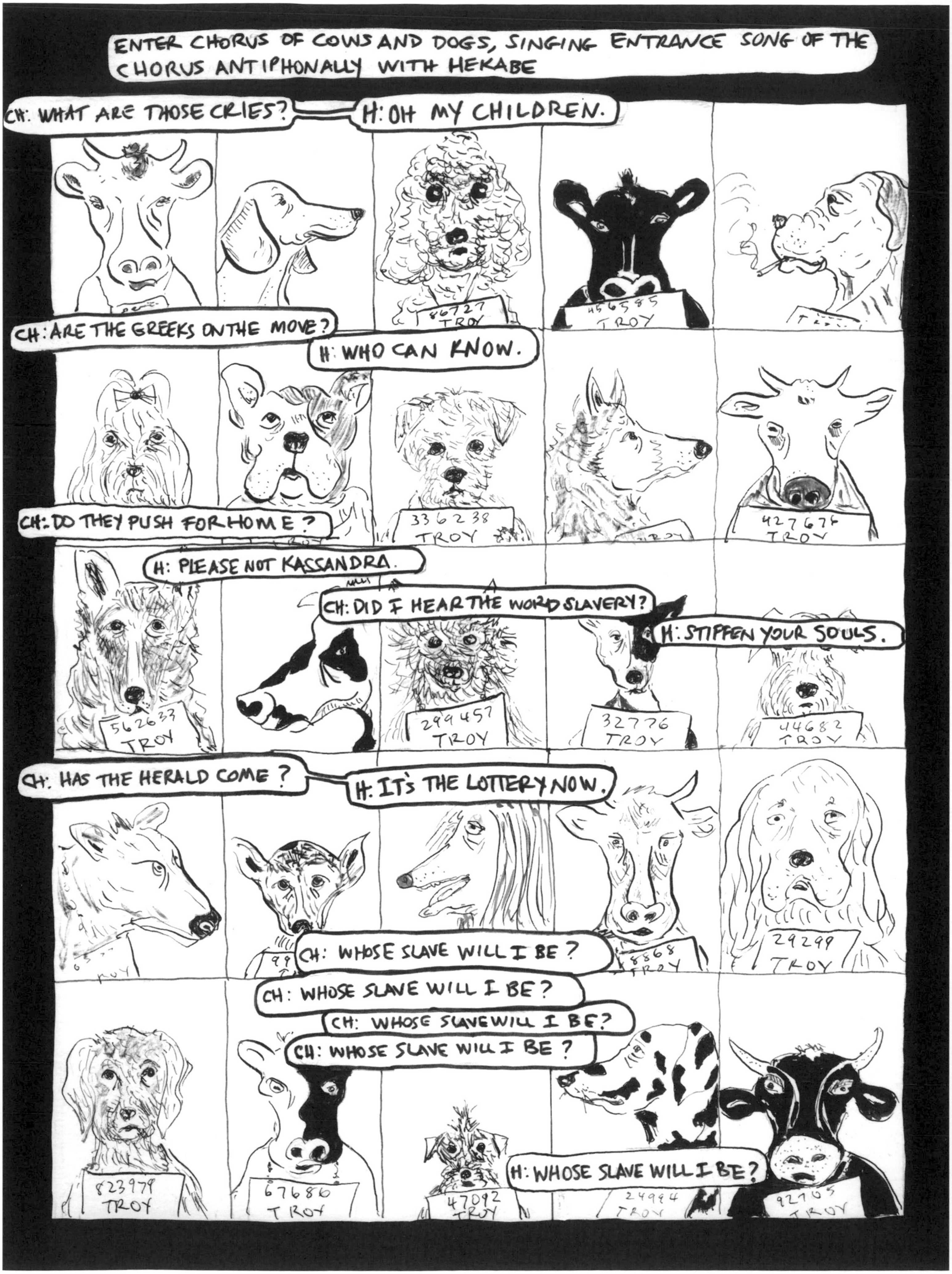

ENTER CHORUS OF COWS AND DOGS, SINGING ENTRANCE SONG OF THE CHORUS ANTIPHONALLY WITH HEKABE
CH: WHAT ARE THOSE CRIES?
H: OH MY CHILDREN.
86727 TROY
456585 TROY
CH: ARE THE GREEKS ON THE MOVE?
H: WHO CAN KNOW.
CH: DO THEY PUSH FOR HOME?
336238 TROY
427676 TROY
H: PLEASE NOT KASSANDRA.
CH: DID I HEAR THE WORD SLAVERY?
H: STIFFEN YOUR SOULS.
562633 TROY
299457 TROY
32776 TROY
44682 TROY
CH: HAS THE HERALD COME?
H: IT'S THE LOTTERY NOW.
CH: WHOSE SLAVE WILL I BE?
29299 TROY
CH: WHOSE SLAVE WILL I BE?
CH: WHOSE SLAVE WILL I BE?
CH: WHOSE SLAVE WILL I BE?
H: WHOSE SLAVE WILL I BE?
823979 TROY
67686 TROY
47092 TROY
24994 TROY
92705 TROY

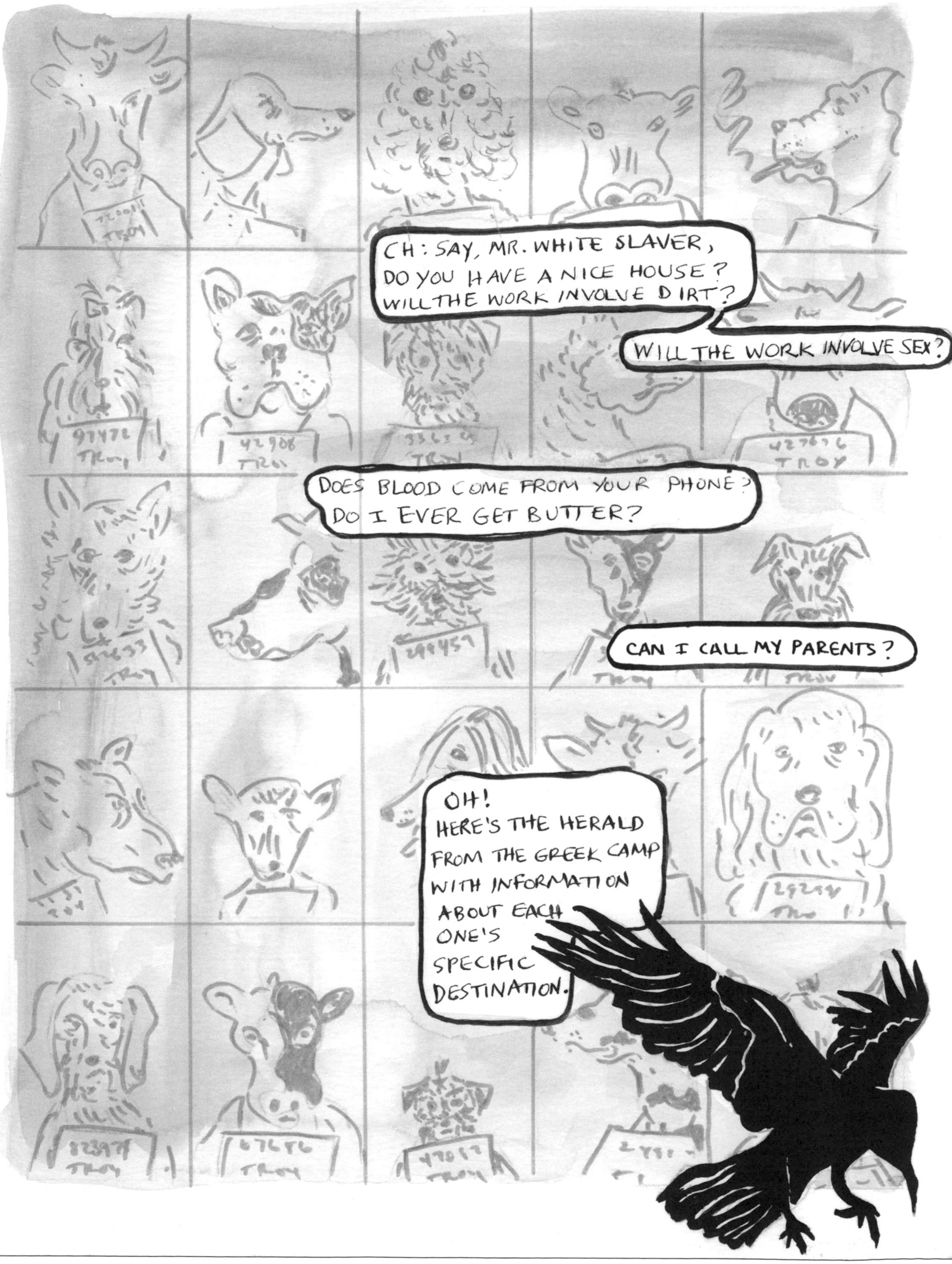
CH: SAY, MR. WHITE SLAVER, DO YOU HAVE A NICE HOUSE? WILL THE WORK INVOLVE DIRT?
WILL THE WORK INVOLVE SEX?
DOES BLOOD COME FROM YOUR PHONE? DO I EVER GET BUTTER?
CAN I CALL MY PARENTS?
OH! HERE'S THE HERALD FROM THE GREEK CAMP WITH INFORMATION ABOUT EACH ONE'S SPECIFIC DESTINATION.

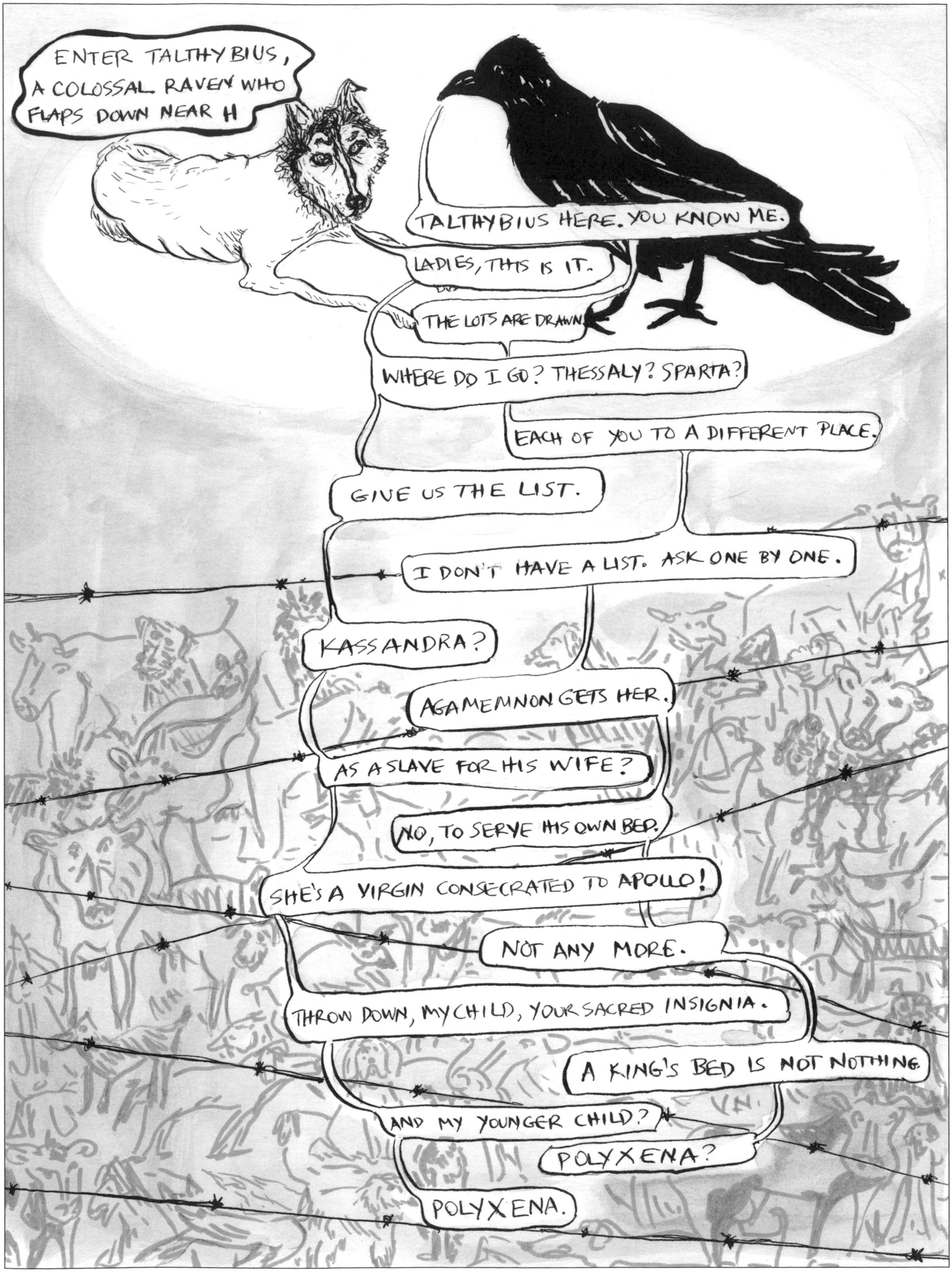
ENTER TALTHYBIUS, A COLOSSAL RAVEN WHO FLAPS DOWN NEAR H
TALTHYBIUS HERE. YOU KNOW ME.
LADIES, THIS IS IT.
THE LOTS ARE DRAWN.
WHERE DO I GO? THESSALY? SPARTA?
EACH OF YOU TO A DIFFERENT PLACE.
GIVE US THE LIST.
I DON'T HAVE A LIST. ASK ONE BY ONE.
KASSANDRA?
AGAMEMNON GETS HER.
AS A SLAVE FOR HIS WIFE?
NO, TO SERVE HIS OWN BED.
SHE'S A VIRGIN CONSECRATED TO APOLLO!
NOT ANY MORE.
THROW DOWN, MY CHILD, YOUR SACRED INSIGNIA.
A KING'S BED IS NOT NOTHING.
AND MY YOUNGER CHILD?
POLYXENA?
POLYXENA.

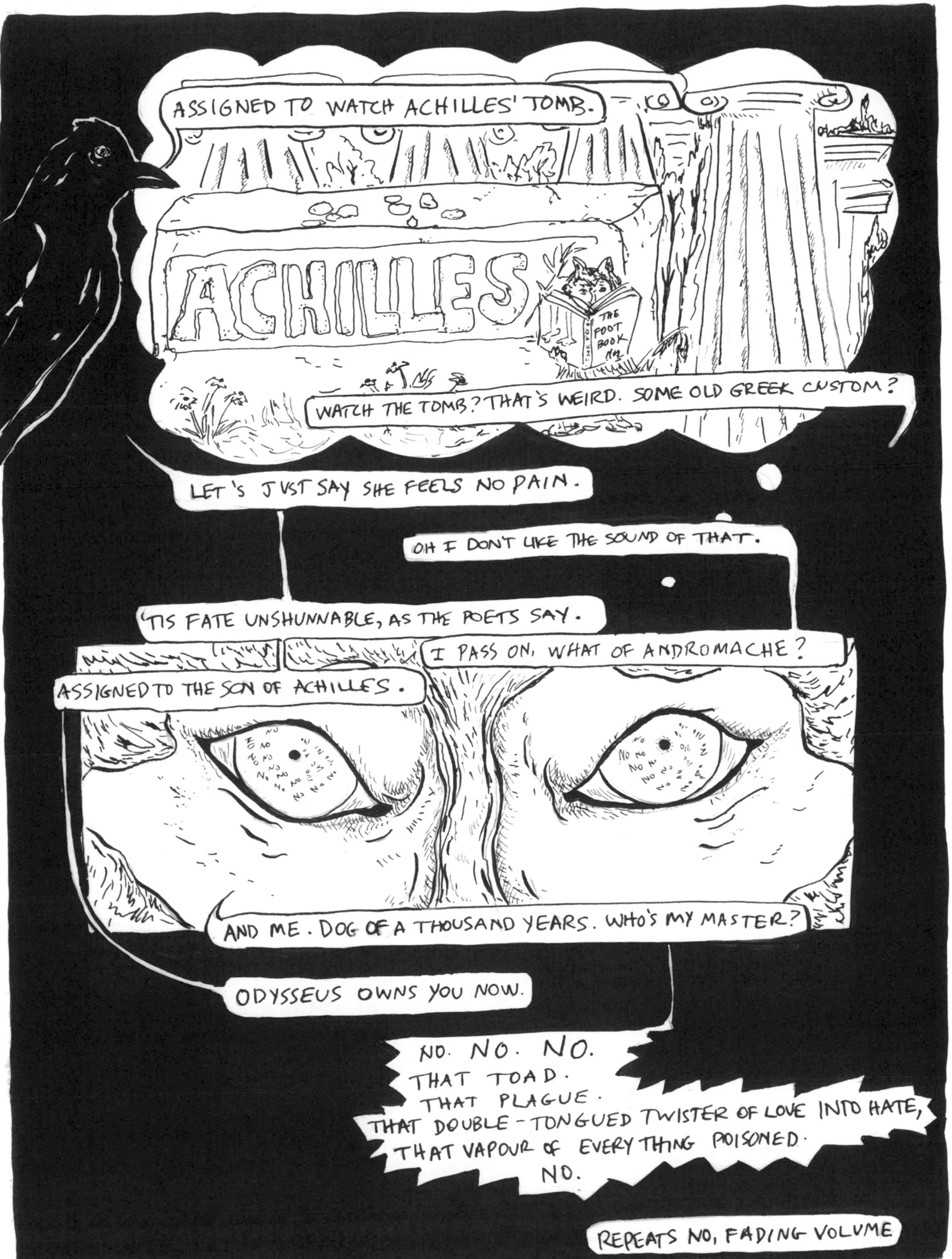
ASSIGNED TO WATCH ACHILLES' TOMB.
ACHILLES
THE FOOT BOOK
WATCH THE TOMB? THAT'S WEIRD. SOME OLD GREEK CUSTOM?
LET'S JUST SAY SHE FEELS NO PAIN.
OH I DON'T LIKE THE SOUND OF THAT.
'TIS FATE UNSHUNNABLE, AS THE POETS SAY.
I PASS ON. WHAT OF ANDROMACHE?
ASSIGNED TO THE SON OF ACHILLES.
AND ME. DOG OF A THOUSAND YEARS. WHO'S MY MASTER?
ODYSSEUS OWNS YOU NOW.
NO. NO. NO. THAT TOAD. THAT PLAGUE. THAT DOUBLE-TONGUED TWISTER OF LOVE INTO HATE, THAT VAPOUR OF EVERYTHING POISONED. NO.
REPEATS NO, FADING VOLUME

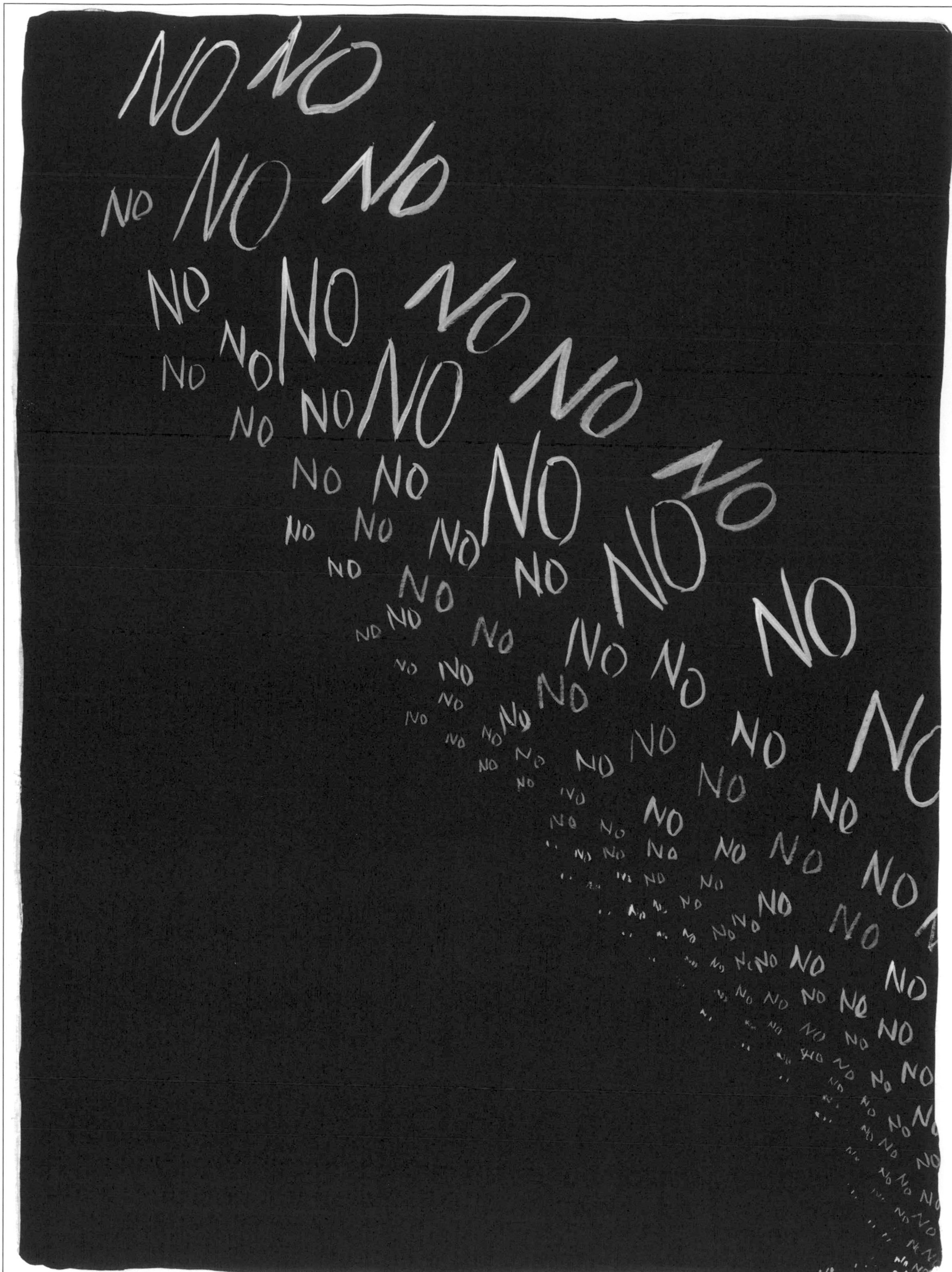

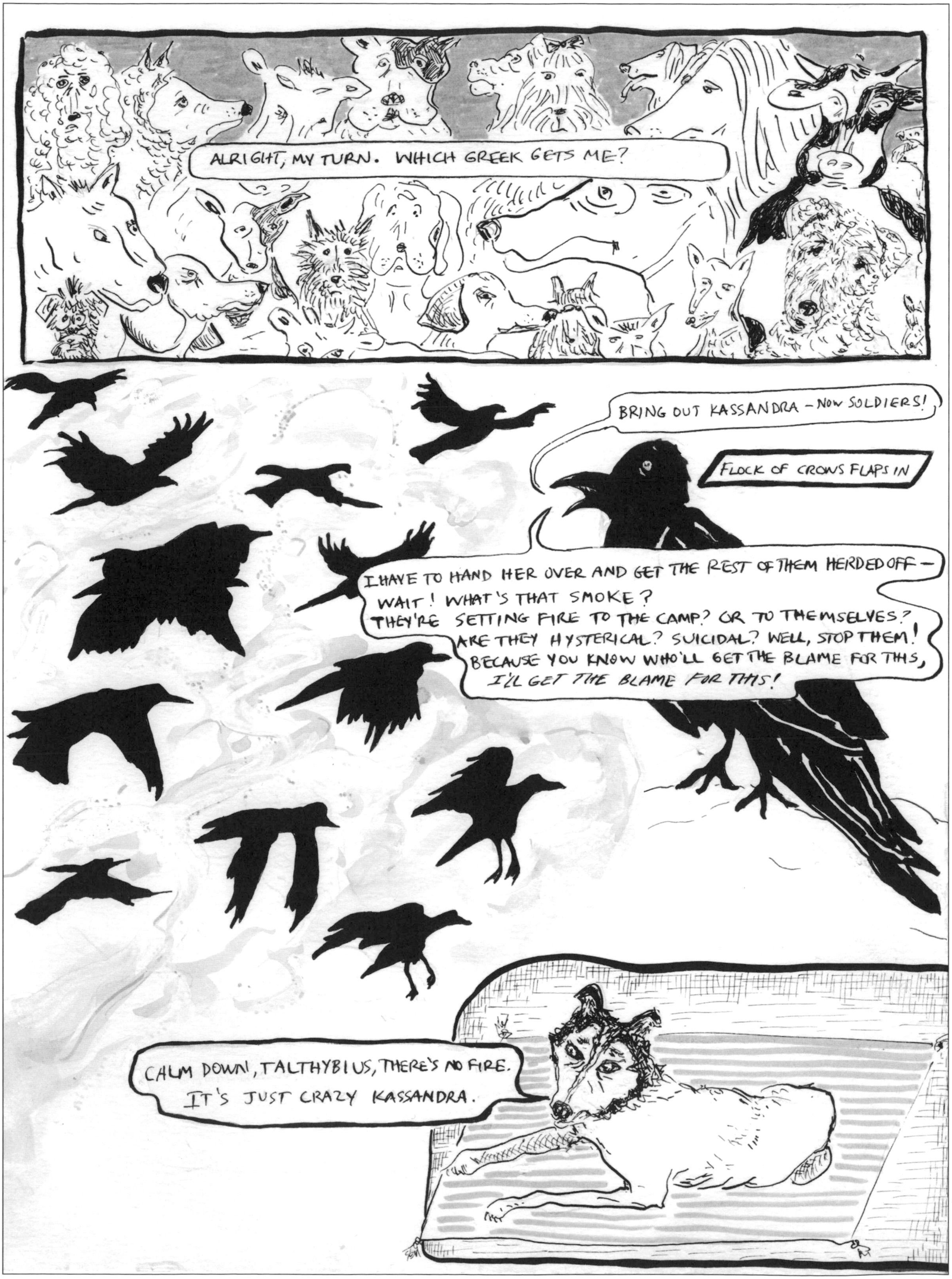
ALRIGHT, MY TURN. WHICH GREEK GETS ME?
BRING OUT KASSANDRA – NOW SOLDIERS!
FLOCK OF CROWS FLAPS IN
I HAVE TO HAND HER OVER AND GET THE REST OF THEM HERDED OFF – WAIT! WHAT'S THAT SMOKE? THEY'RE SETTING FIRE TO THE CAMP? OR TO THEMSELVES? ARE THEY HYSTERICAL? SUICIDAL? WELL, STOP THEM! BECAUSE YOU KNOW WHO'LL GET THE BLAME FOR THIS, I'LL GET THE BLAME FOR THIS!
CALM DOWN, TALTHYBIUS, THERE'S NO FIRE. IT'S JUST CRAZY KASSANDRA.

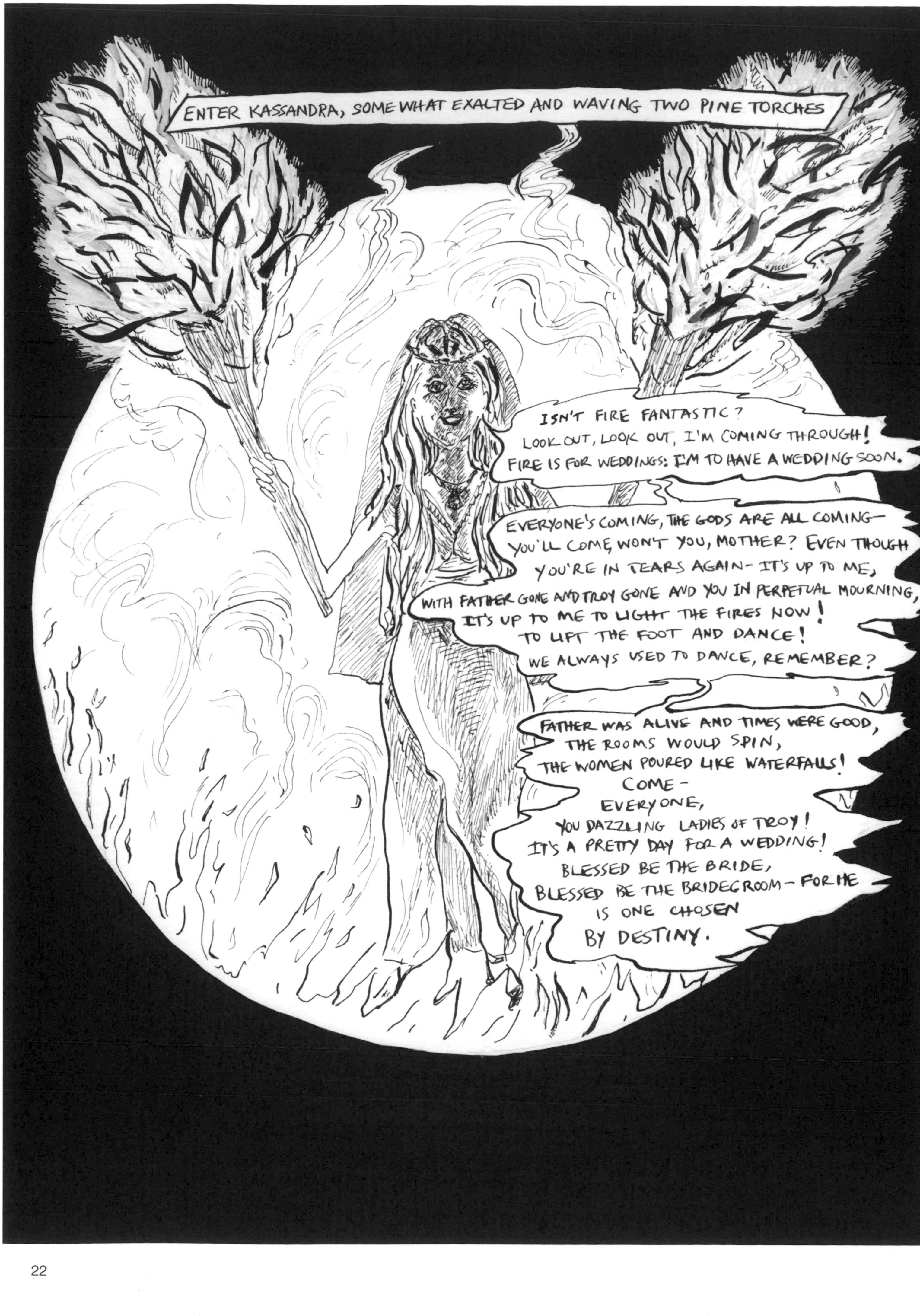
ENTER KASSANDRA, SOME WHAT EXALTED AND WAVING TWO PINE TORCHES
ISN'T FIRE FANTASTIC? LOOK OUT, LOOK OUT, I'M COMING THROUGH! FIRE IS FOR WEDDINGS: I'M TO HAVE A WEDDING SOON.
EVERYONE'S COMING, THE GODS ARE ALL COMING— YOU'LL COME, WON'T YOU, MOTHER? EVEN THOUGH YOU'RE IN TEARS AGAIN— IT'S UP TO ME, WITH FATHER GONE AND TROY GONE AND YOU IN PERPETUAL MOURNING, IT'S UP TO ME TO LIGHT THE FIRES NOW! TO LIFT THE FOOT AND DANCE! WE ALWAYS USED TO DANCE, REMEMBER?
FATHER WAS ALIVE AND TIMES WERE GOOD, THE ROOMS WOULD SPIN, THE WOMEN POURED LIKE WATERFALLS! COME— EVERYONE, YOU DAZZLING LADIES OF TROY! IT'S A PRETTY DAY FOR A WEDDING! BLESSED BE THE BRIDE, BLESSED BE THE BRIDEGROOM— FOR HE IS ONE CHOSEN BY DESTINY.

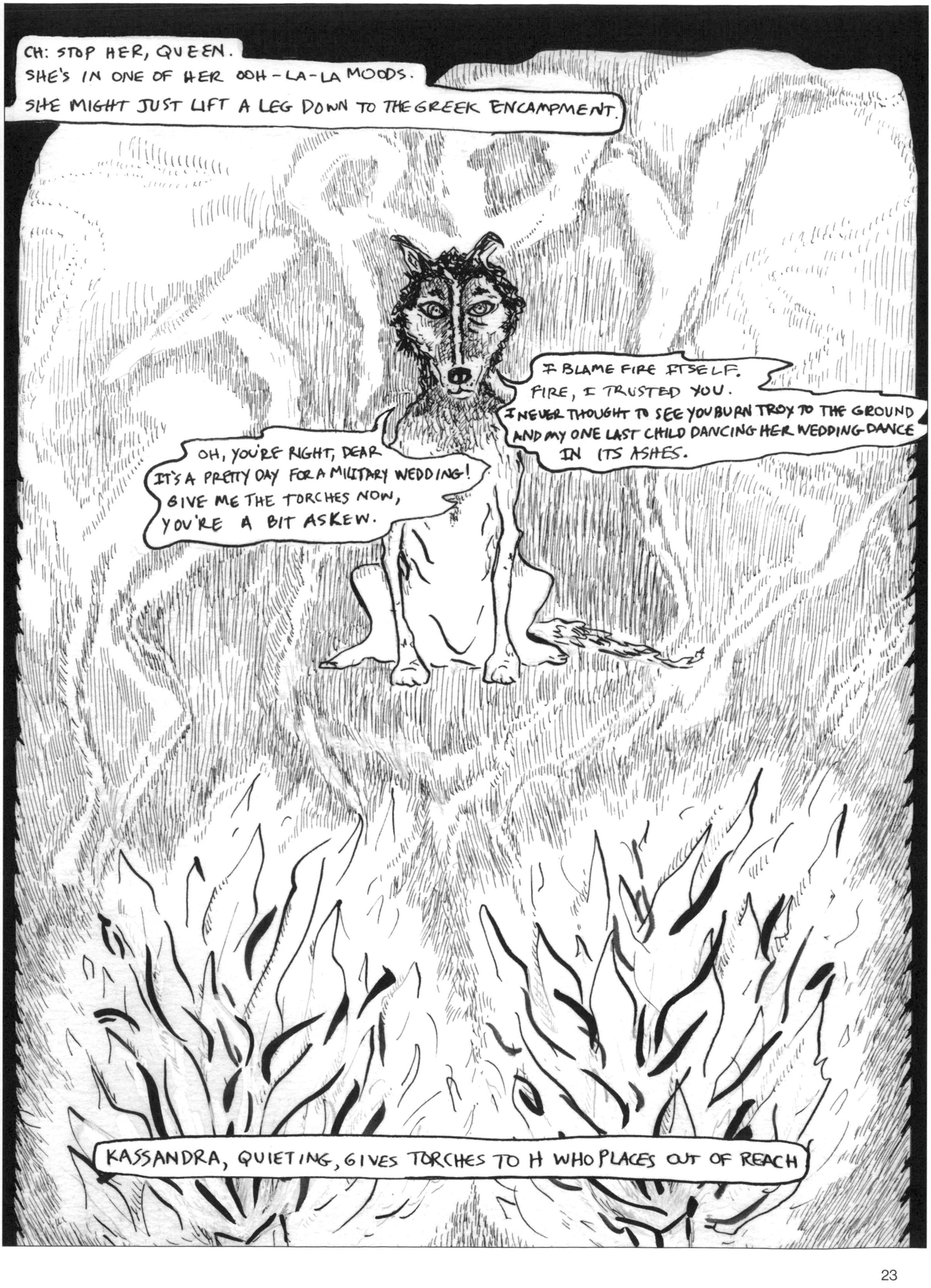
CH: STOP HER, QUEEN.
SHE'S IN ONE OF HER OOH-LA-LA MOODS.
SHE MIGHT JUST LIFT A LEG DOWN TO THE GREEK ENCAMPMENT.
I BLAME FIRE ITSELF.
FIRE, I TRUSTED YOU.
I NEVER THOUGHT TO SEE YOU BURN TROY TO THE GROUND
AND MY ONE LAST CHILD DANCING HER WEDDING DANCE
IN ITS ASHES.
OH, YOU'RE RIGHT, DEAR
IT'S A PRETTY DAY FOR A MILITARY WEDDING!
GIVE ME THE TORCHES NOW,
YOU'RE A BIT ASKEW.
KASSANDRA, QUIETING, GIVES TORCHES TO H WHO PLACES OUT OF REACH

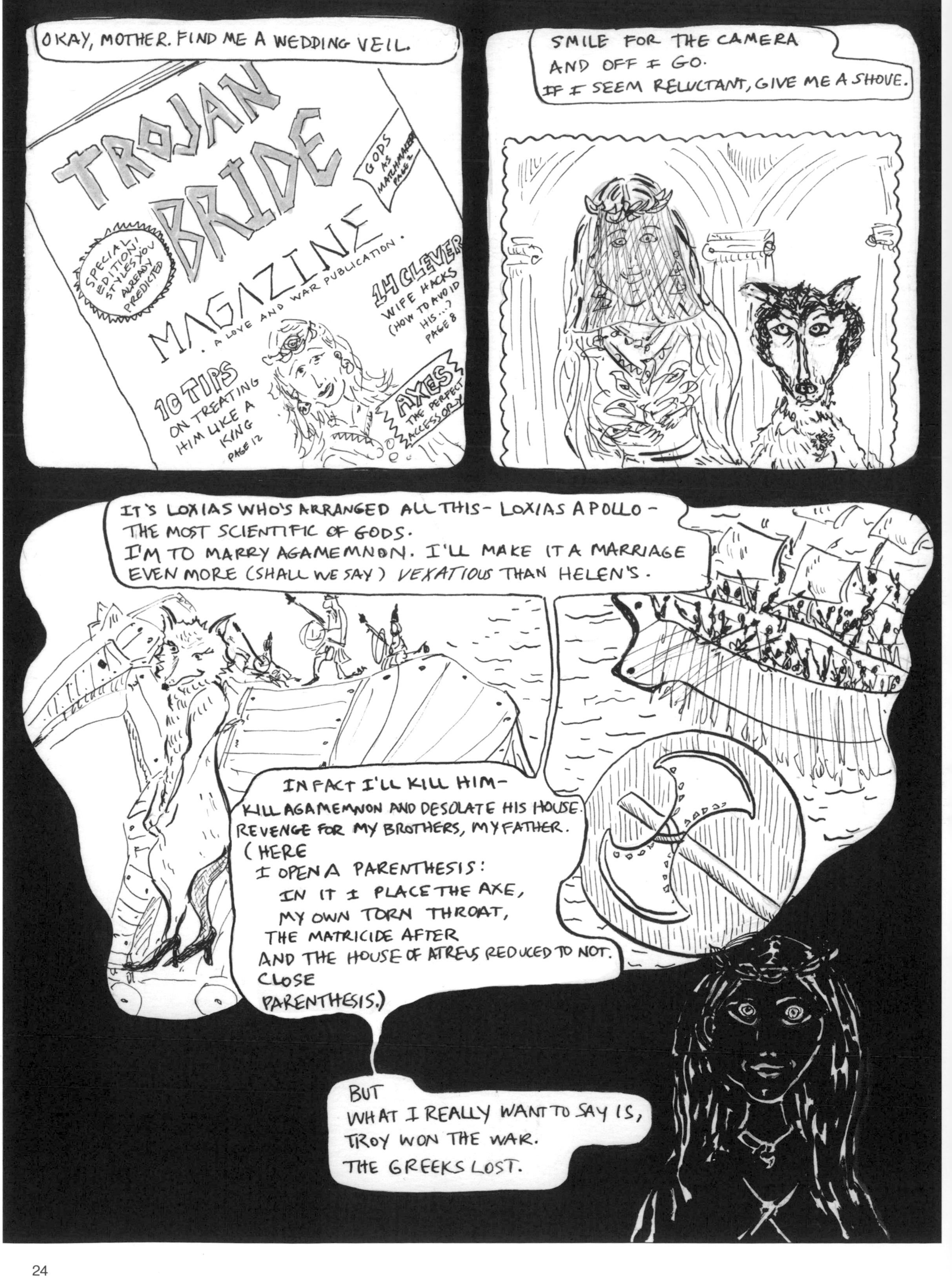
OKAY, MOTHER. FIND ME A WEDDING VEIL.
TROJAN BRIDE
GODS AS MATCHMAKERS PAGE 2
SPECIAL EDITION! STYLES YOU ALREADY PREDICTED
MAGAZINE
A LOVE AND WAR PUBLICATION.
14 CLEVER WIFE HACKS (HOW TO AVOID HIS...? PAGE 8
10 TIPS ON TREATING HIM LIKE A KING PAGE 12
AXES THE PERFECT ACCESSORY
SMILE FOR THE CAMERA AND OFF I GO. IF I SEEM RELUCTANT, GIVE ME A SHOVE.
IT'S LOXIAS WHO'S ARRANGED ALL THIS- LOXIAS APOLLO- THE MOST SCIENTIFIC OF GODS. I'M TO MARRY AGAMEMNON. I'LL MAKE IT A MARRIAGE EVEN MORE (SHALL WE SAY) *VEXATIOUS* THAN HELEN'S.
IN FACT I'LL KILL HIM- KILL AGAMEMNON AND DESOLATE HIS HOUSE. REVENGE FOR MY BROTHERS, MY FATHER. (HERE I OPEN A PARENTHESIS: IN IT I PLACE THE AXE, MY OWN TORN THROAT, THE MATRICIDE AFTER AND THE HOUSE OF ATREUS REDUCED TO NOT. CLOSE PARENTHESIS.)
BUT WHAT I REALLY WANT TO SAY IS, TROY WON THE WAR. THE GREEKS LOST.

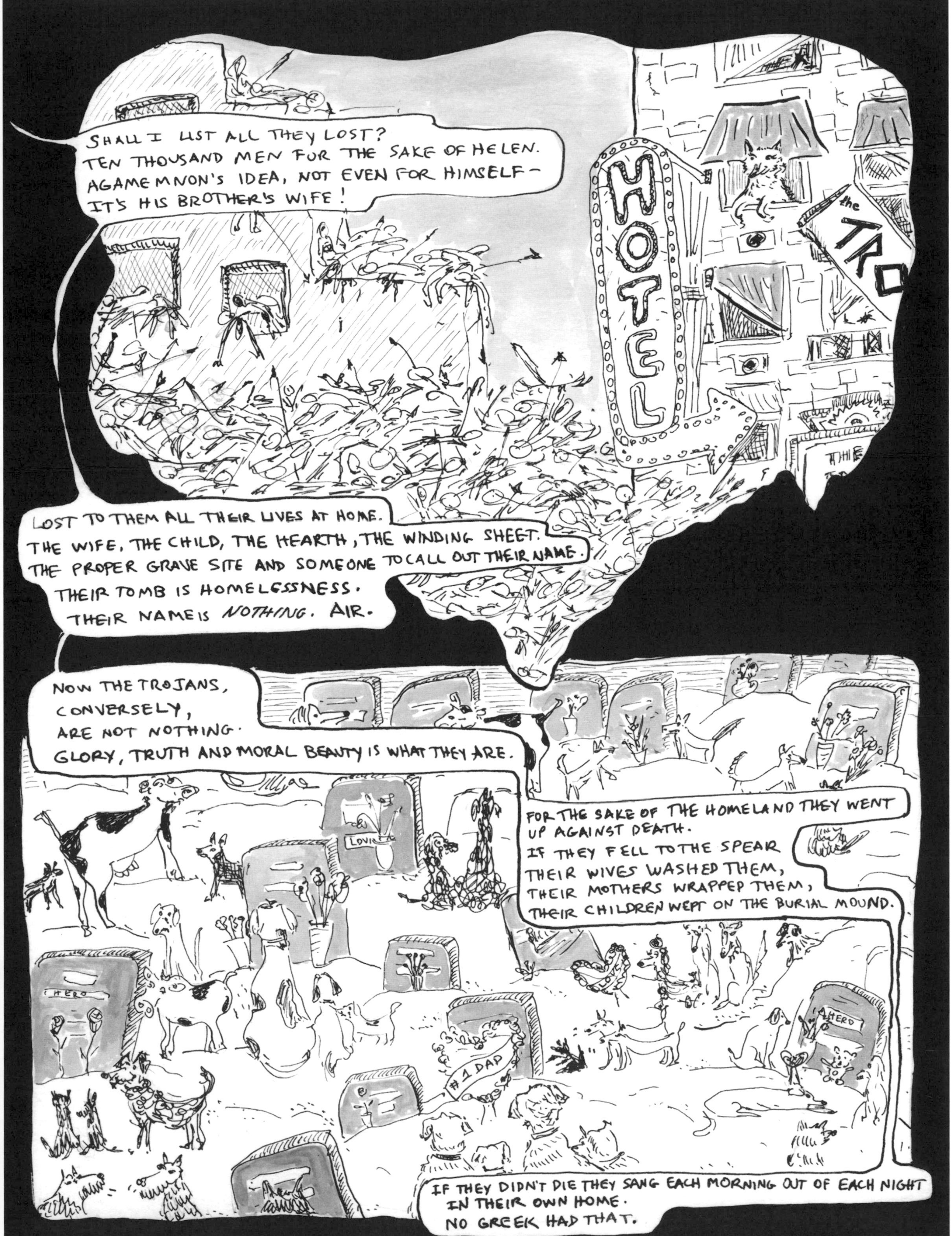
SHALL I LIST ALL THEY LOST?
TEN THOUSAND MEN FOR THE SAKE OF HELEN.
AGAMEMNON'S IDEA, NOT EVEN FOR HIMSELF—
IT'S HIS BROTHER'S WIFE!
HOTEL
the TRO
LOST TO THEM ALL THEIR LIVES AT HOME.
THE WIFE, THE CHILD, THE HEARTH, THE WINDING SHEET.
THE PROPER GRAVE SITE AND SOMEONE TO CALL OUT THEIR NAME.
THEIR TOMB IS HOMELESSNESS.
THEIR NAME IS NOTHING. AIR.
NOW THE TROJANS,
CONVERSELY,
ARE NOT NOTHING.
GLORY, TRUTH AND MORAL BEAUTY IS WHAT THEY ARE.
FOR THE SAKE OF THE HOMELAND THEY WENT UP AGAINST DEATH.
IF THEY FELL TO THE SPEAR
THEIR WIVES WASHED THEM,
THEIR MOTHERS WRAPPED THEM,
THEIR CHILDREN WEPT ON THE BURIAL MOUND.
HERO
HERO
#1 DAD
IF THEY DIDN'T DIE THEY SANG EACH MORNING OUT OF EACH NIGHT
IN THEIR OWN HOME.
NO GREEK HAD THAT.

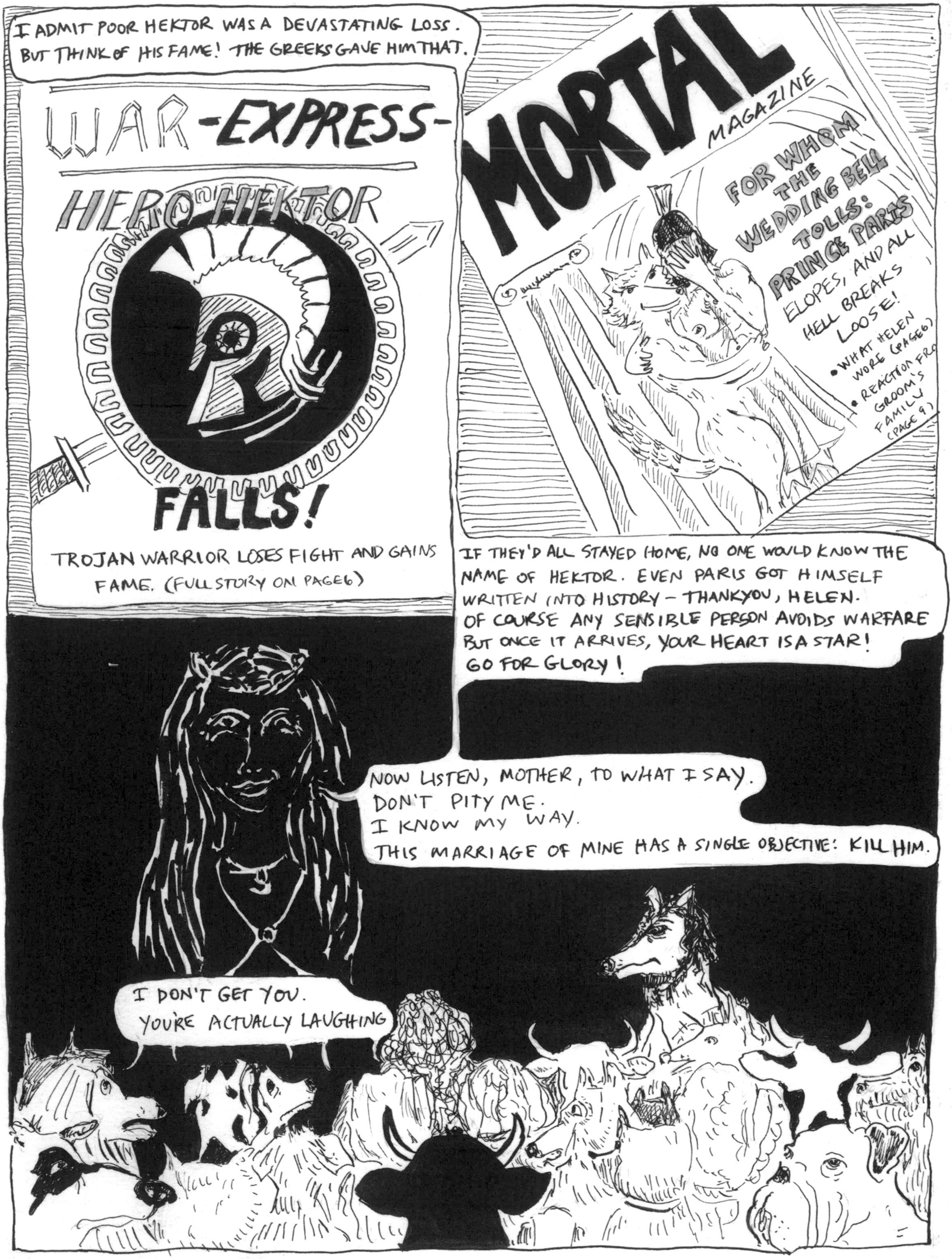
I ADMIT POOR HEKTOR WAS A DEVASTATING LOSS.
BUT THINK OF HIS FAME! THE GREEKS GAVE HIM THAT.
WAR -EXPRESS-
HERO HEKTOR
FALLS!
TROJAN WARRIOR LOSES FIGHT AND GAINS FAME. (FULL STORY ON PAGE6)
MORTAL
MAGAZINE
FOR WHOM THE WEDDING BELL TOLLS: PRINCE PARIS ELOPES, AND ALL HELL BREAKS LOOSE!
• WHAT HELEN WORE (PAGE6)
• REACTION FRO GROOM'S FAMILY (PAGE 9)
IF THEY'D ALL STAYED HOME, NO ONE WOULD KNOW THE NAME OF HEKTOR. EVEN PARIS GOT HIMSELF WRITTEN INTO HISTORY – THANKYOU, HELEN.
OF COURSE ANY SENSIBLE PERSON AVOIDS WARFARE
BUT ONCE IT ARRIVES, YOUR HEART IS A STAR!
GO FOR GLORY!
NOW LISTEN, MOTHER, TO WHAT I SAY.
DON'T PITY ME.
I KNOW MY WAY.
THIS MARRIAGE OF MINE HAS A SINGLE OBJECTIVE: KILL HIM.
I DON'T GET YOU.
YOU'RE ACTUALLY LAUGHING

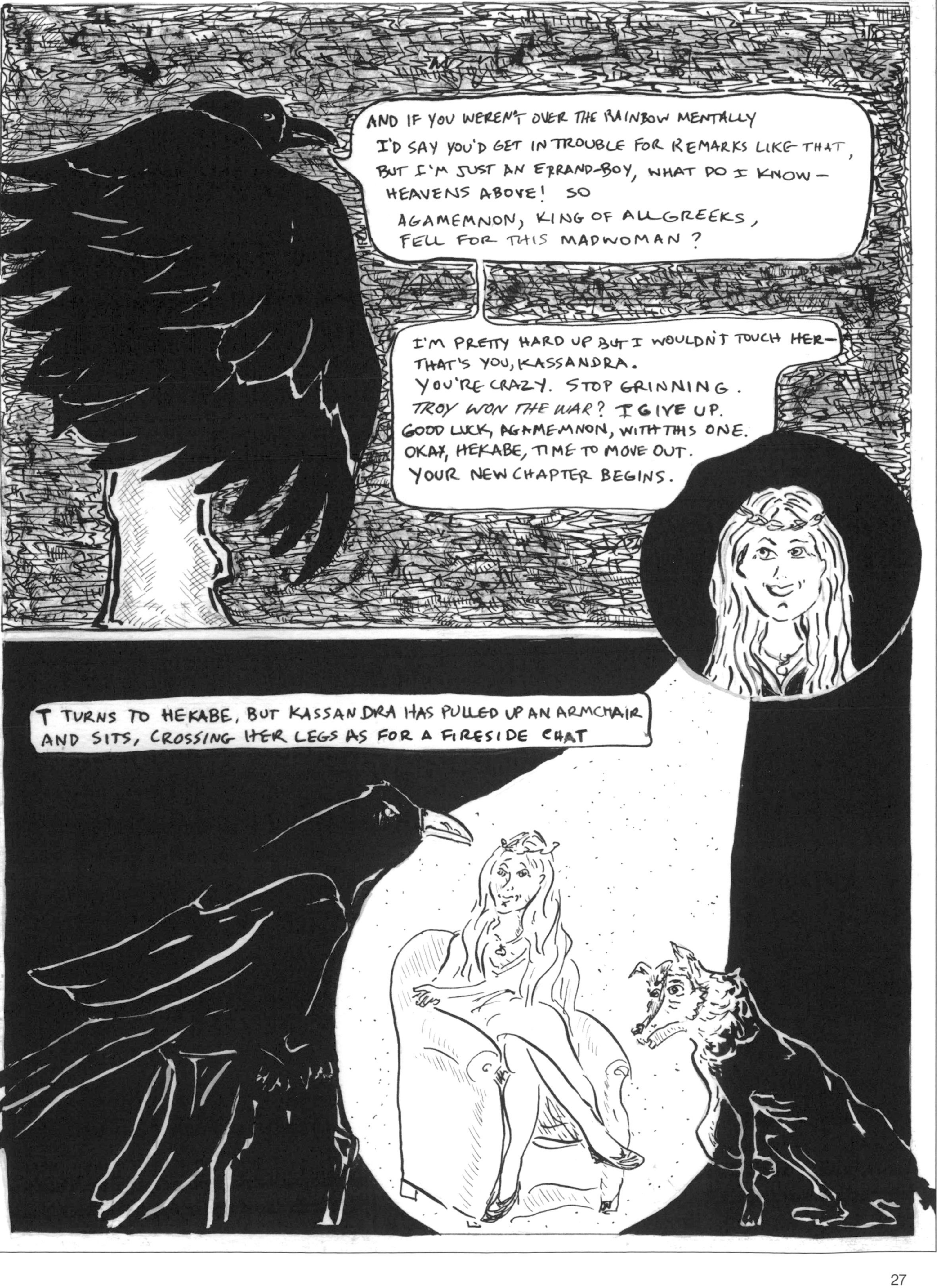
AND IF YOU WEREN'T OVER THE RAINBOW MENTALLY I'D SAY YOU'D GET IN TROUBLE FOR REMARKS LIKE THAT, BUT I'M JUST AN ERRAND-BOY, WHAT DO I KNOW – HEAVENS ABOVE! SO AGAMEMNON, KING OF ALL GREEKS, FELL FOR THIS MADWOMAN?
I'M PRETTY HARD UP BUT I WOULDN'T TOUCH HER – THAT'S YOU, KASSANDRA. YOU'RE CRAZY. STOP GRINNING. TROY WON THE WAR? I GIVE UP. GOOD LUCK, AGAMEMNON, WITH THIS ONE. OKAY, HEKABE, TIME TO MOVE OUT. YOUR NEW CHAPTER BEGINS.
T TURNS TO HEKABE, BUT KASSANDRA HAS PULLED UP AN ARMCHAIR AND SITS, CROSSING HER LEGS AS FOR A FIRESIDE CHAT

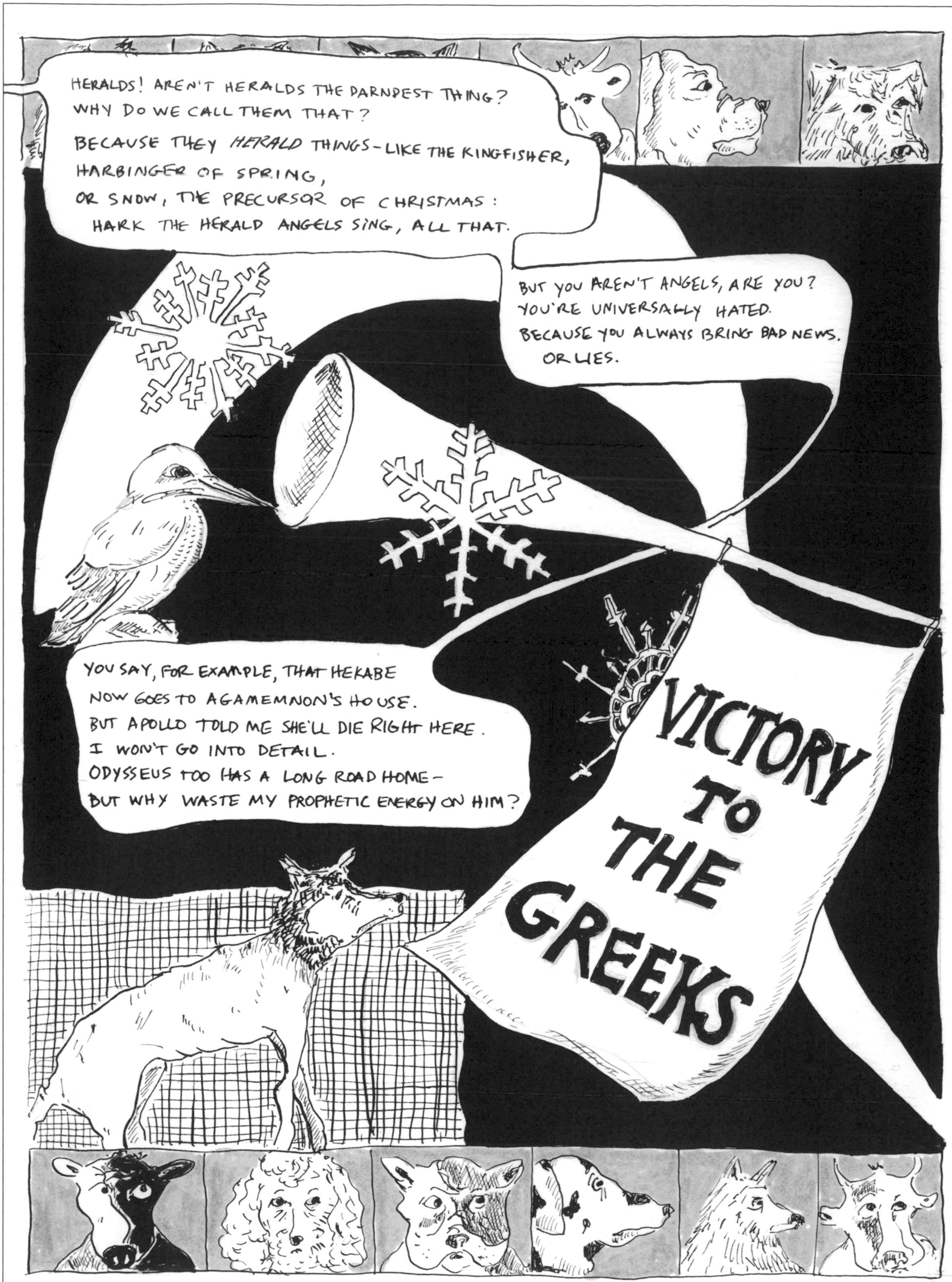
HERALDS! AREN'T HERALDS THE DARNDEST THING? WHY DO WE CALL THEM THAT? BECAUSE THEY *HERALD* THINGS—LIKE THE KINGFISHER, HARBINGER OF SPRING, OR SNOW, THE PRECURSOR OF CHRISTMAS: HARK THE HERALD ANGELS SING, ALL THAT.
BUT YOU AREN'T ANGELS, ARE YOU? YOU'RE UNIVERSALLY HATED. BECAUSE YOU ALWAYS BRING BAD NEWS. OR LIES.
YOU SAY, FOR EXAMPLE, THAT HEKABE NOW GOES TO AGAMEMNON'S HOUSE. BUT APOLLO TOLD ME SHE'LL DIE RIGHT HERE. I WON'T GO INTO DETAIL. ODYSSEUS TOO HAS A LONG ROAD HOME— BUT WHY WASTE MY PROPHETIC ENERGY ON HIM?
VICTORY TO THE GREEKS

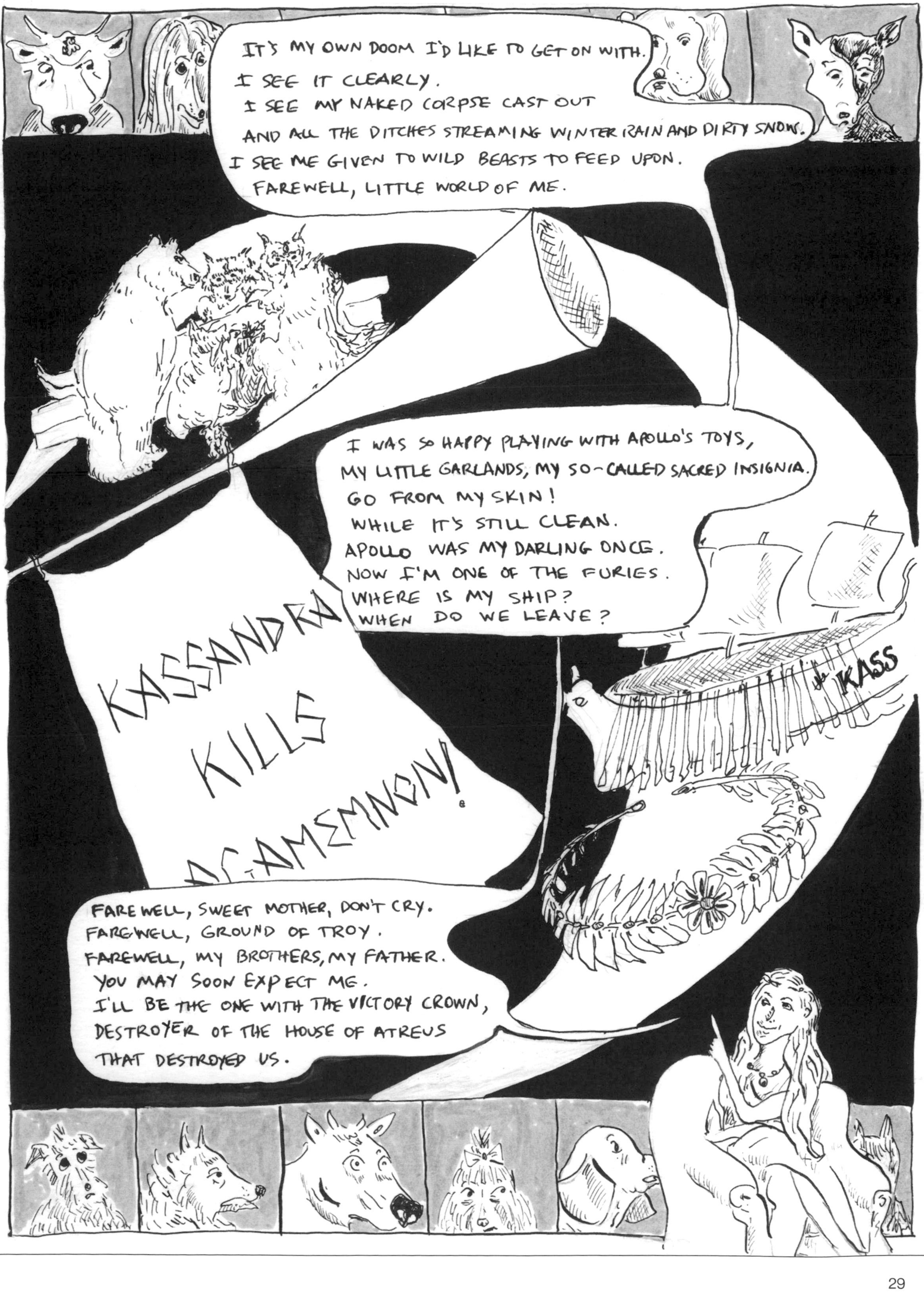
IT'S MY OWN DOOM I'D LIKE TO GET ON WITH.
I SEE IT CLEARLY.
I SEE MY NAKED CORPSE CAST OUT
AND ALL THE DITCHES STREAMING WINTER RAIN AND DIRTY SNOW.
I SEE ME GIVEN TO WILD BEASTS TO FEED UPON.
FAREWELL, LITTLE WORLD OF ME.
I WAS SO HAPPY PLAYING WITH APOLLO'S TOYS,
MY LITTLE GARLANDS, MY SO-CALLED SACRED INSIGNIA.
GO FROM MY SKIN!
WHILE IT'S STILL CLEAN.
APOLLO WAS MY DARLING ONCE.
NOW I'M ONE OF THE FURIES.
WHERE IS MY SHIP?
WHEN DO WE LEAVE?
KASSANDRA KILLS AGAMEMNON!
KASS
FAREWELL, SWEET MOTHER, DON'T CRY.
FAREWELL, GROUND OF TROY.
FAREWELL, MY BROTHERS, MY FATHER.
YOU MAY SOON EXPECT ME.
I'LL BE THE ONE WITH THE VICTORY CROWN,
DESTROYER OF THE HOUSE OF ATREUS
THAT DESTROYED US.

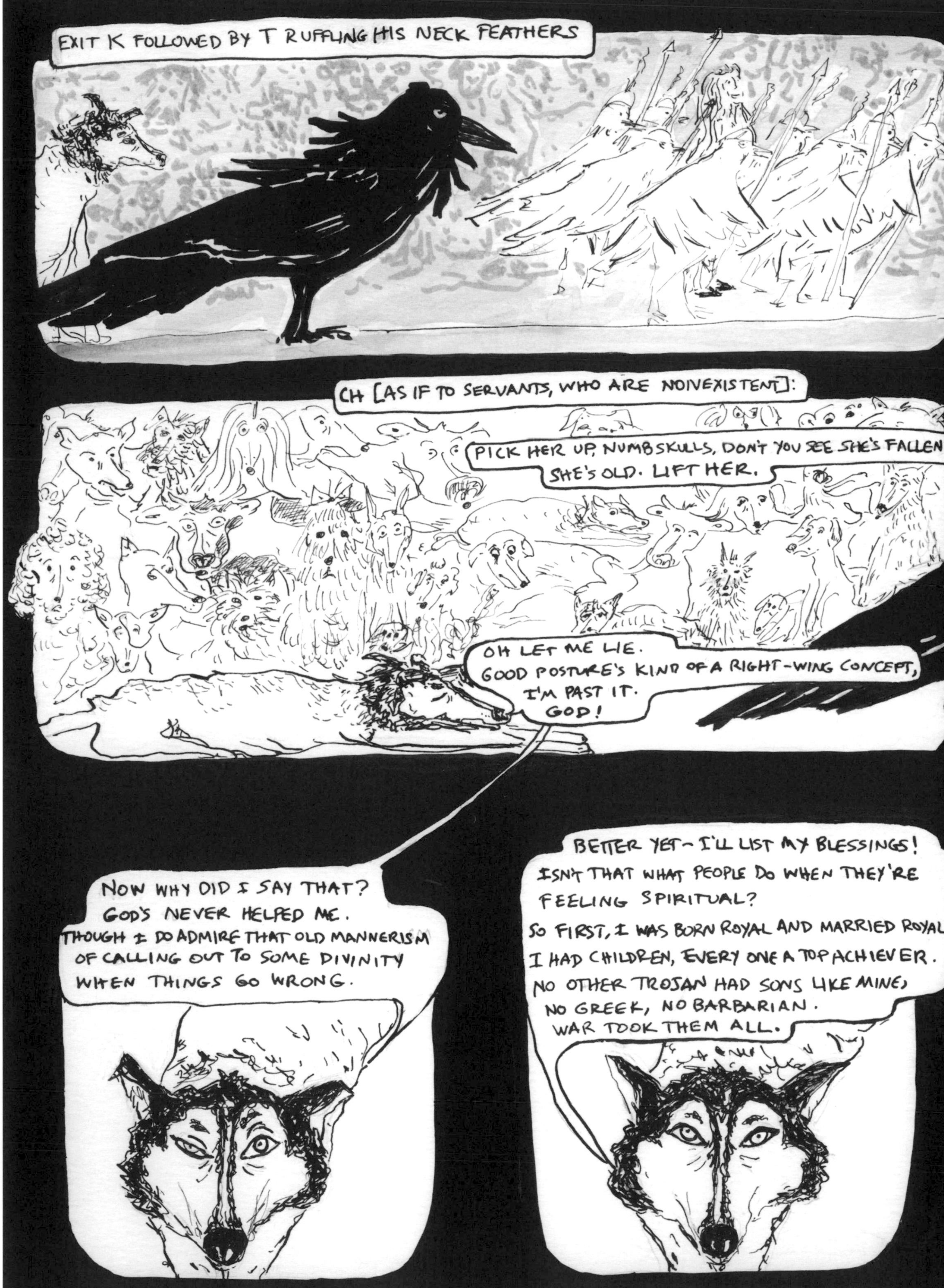
EXIT K FOLLOWED BY T RUFFLING HIS NECK FEATHERS
CH [AS IF TO SERVANTS, WHO ARE NONEXISTENT]:
PICK HER UP, NUMBSKULLS, DON'T YOU SEE SHE'S FALLEN? SHE'S OLD. LIFT HER.
OH LET ME LIE. GOOD POSTURE'S KIND OF A RIGHT-WING CONCEPT, I'M PAST IT. GOD!
NOW WHY DID I SAY THAT? GOD'S NEVER HELPED ME. THOUGH I DO ADMIRE THAT OLD MANNERISM OF CALLING OUT TO SOME DIVINITY WHEN THINGS GO WRONG.
BETTER YET - I'LL LIST MY BLESSINGS! ISN'T THAT WHAT PEOPLE DO WHEN THEY'RE FEELING SPIRITUAL? SO FIRST, I WAS BORN ROYAL AND MARRIED ROYAL. I HAD CHILDREN, EVERY ONE A TOP ACHIEVER. NO OTHER TROJAN HAD SONS LIKE MINE, NO GREEK, NO BARBARIAN. WAR TOOK THEM ALL.

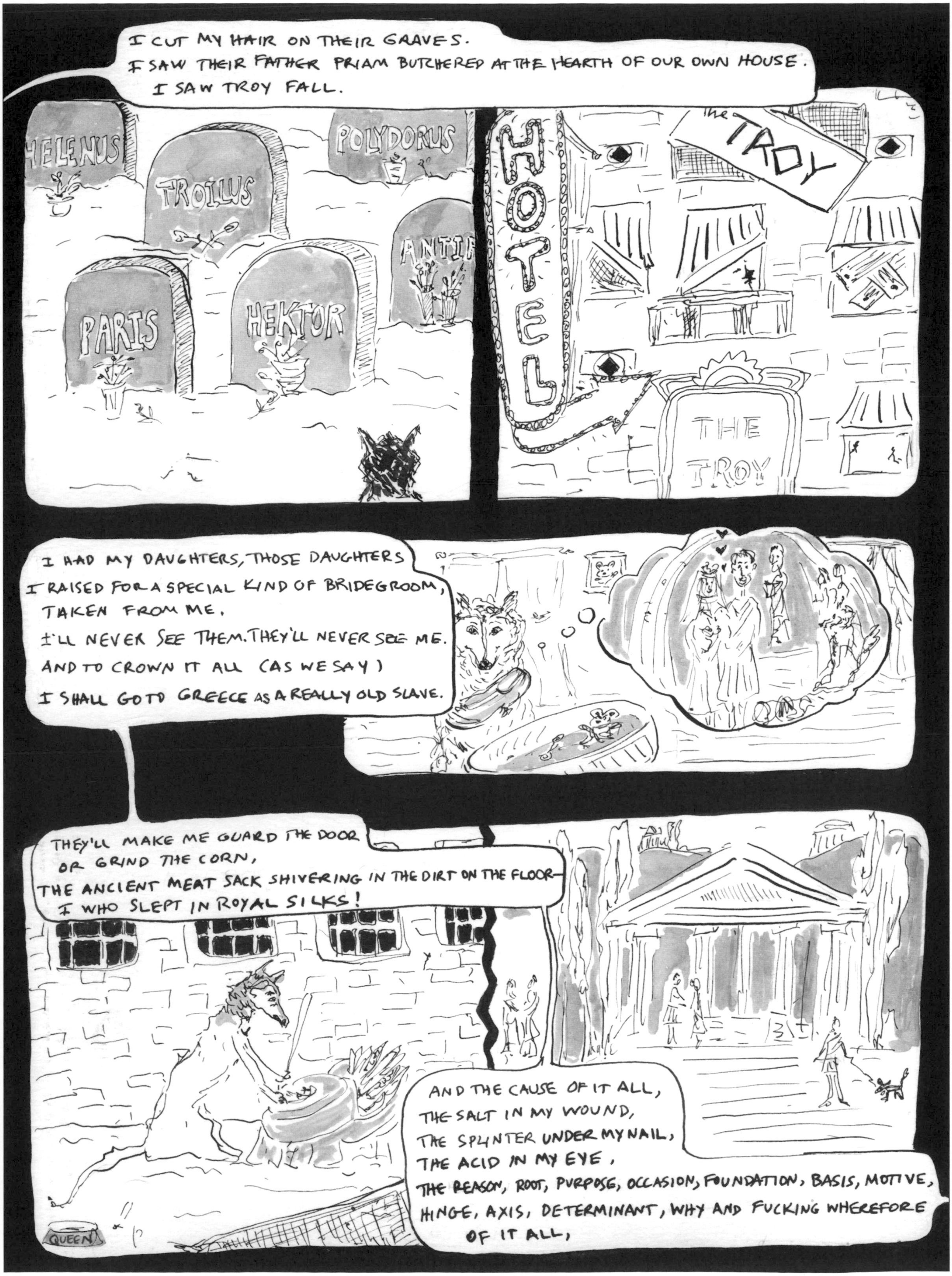
I CUT MY HAIR ON THEIR GRAVES.
I SAW THEIR FATHER PRIAM BUTCHERED AT THE HEARTH OF OUR OWN HOUSE.
I SAW TROY FALL.
HELENUS
POLYDORUS
TROILUS
PARIS
HEKTOR
HOTEL
THE TROY
THE TROY
I HAD MY DAUGHTERS, THOSE DAUGHTERS
I RAISED FOR A SPECIAL KIND OF BRIDEGROOM,
TAKEN FROM ME.
I'LL NEVER SEE THEM. THEY'LL NEVER SEE ME.
AND TO CROWN IT ALL (AS WE SAY)
I SHALL GO TO GREECE AS A REALLY OLD SLAVE.
THEY'LL MAKE ME GUARD THE DOOR
OR GRIND THE CORN,
THE ANCIENT MEAT SACK SHIVERING IN THE DIRT ON THE FLOOR—
I WHO SLEPT IN ROYAL SILKS!
QUEEN
AND THE CAUSE OF IT ALL,
THE SALT IN MY WOUND,
THE SPLINTER UNDER MY NAIL,
THE ACID IN MY EYE,
THE REASON, ROOT, PURPOSE, OCCASION, FOUNDATION, BASIS, MOTIVE,
HINGE, AXIS, DETERMINANT, WHY AND FUCKING WHEREFORE
OF IT ALL,

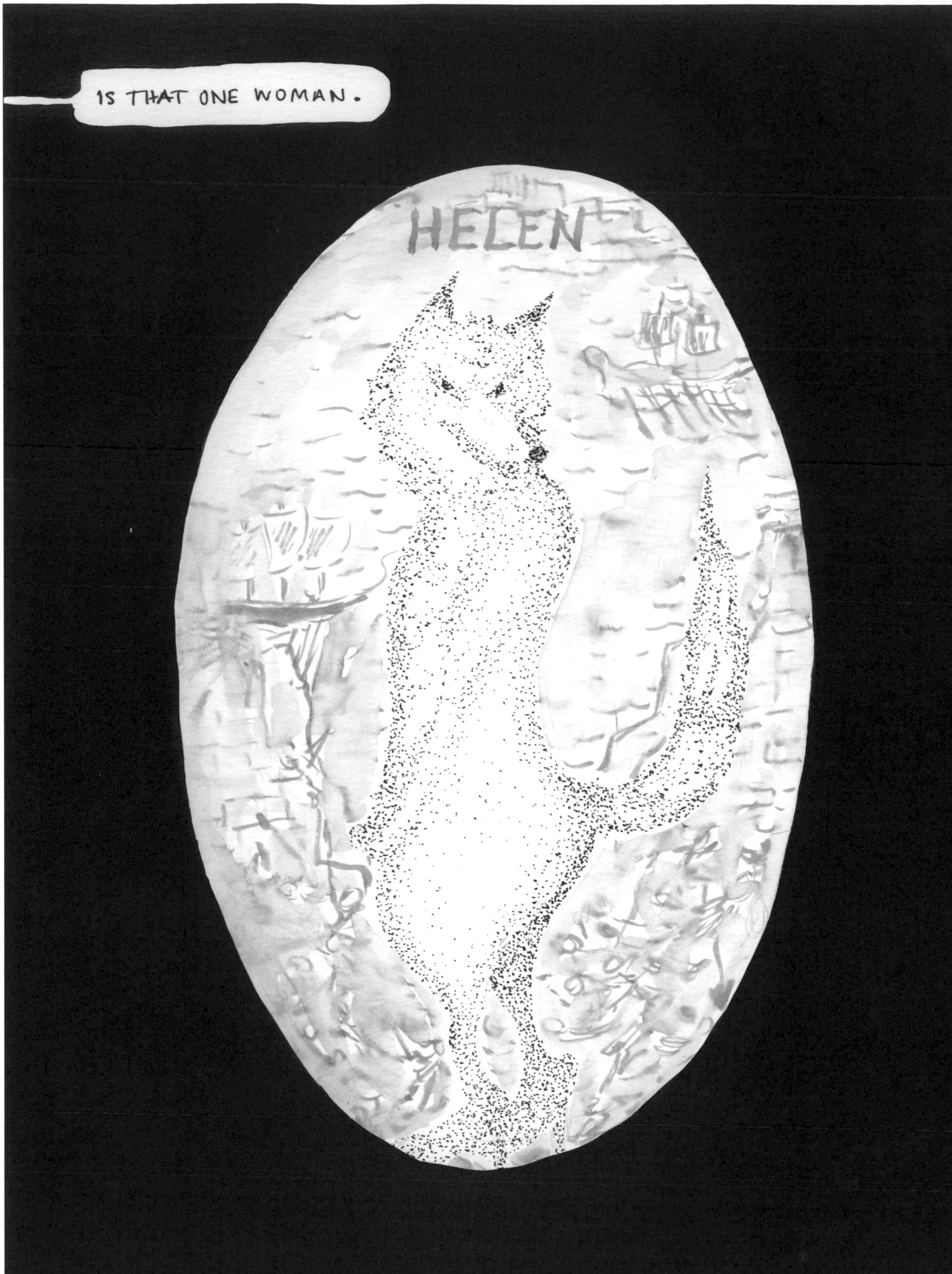
IS THAT ONE WOMAN.
HELEN

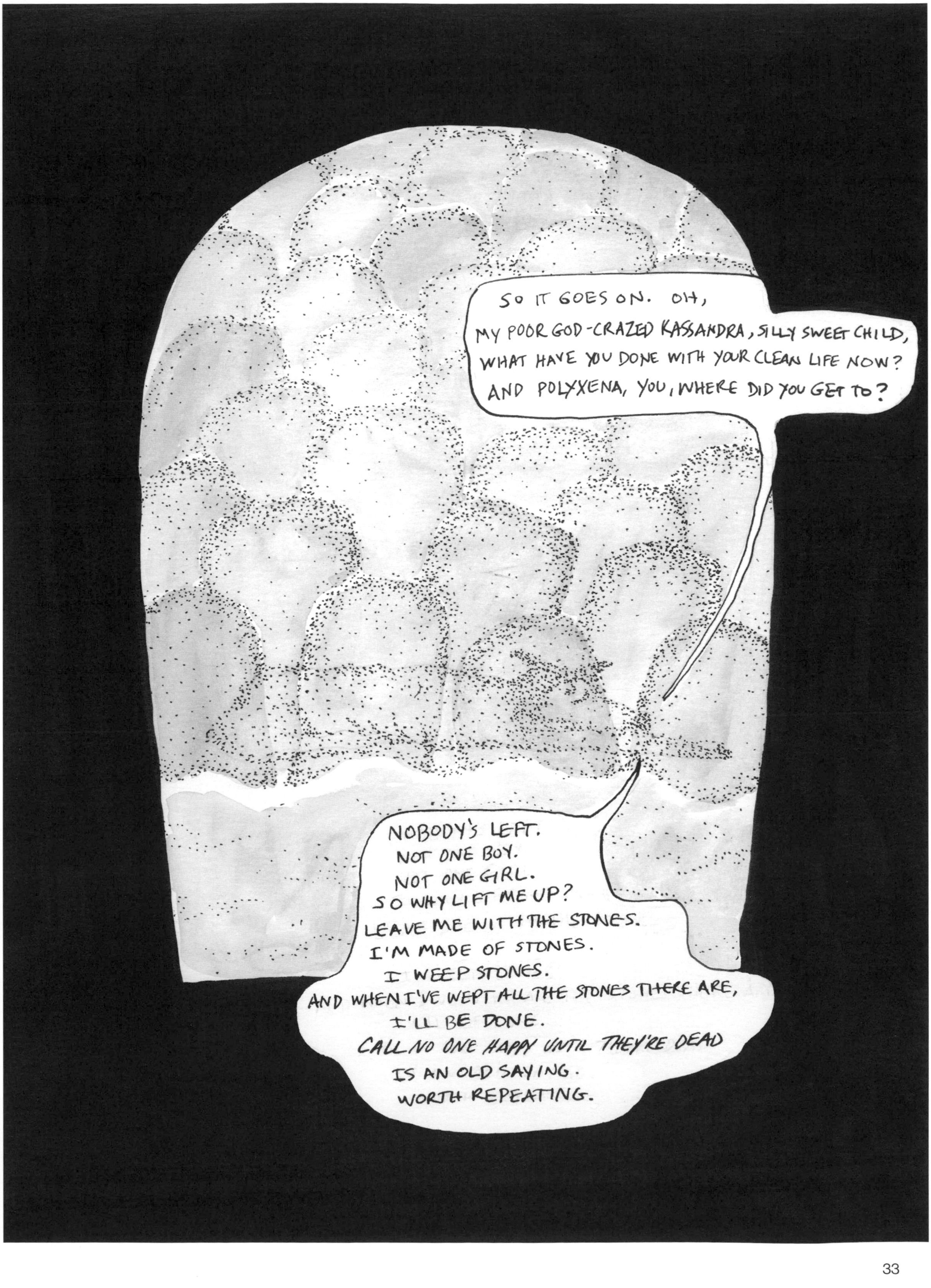
SO IT GOES ON. OH, MY POOR GOD-CRAZED KASSANDRA, SILLY SWEET CHILD, WHAT HAVE YOU DONE WITH YOUR CLEAN LIFE NOW? AND POLYXENA, YOU, WHERE DID YOU GET TO?
NOBODY'S LEFT. NOT ONE BOY. NOT ONE GIRL. SO WHY LIFT ME UP? LEAVE ME WITH THE STONES. I'M MADE OF STONES. I WEEP STONES. AND WHEN I'VE WEPT ALL THE STONES THERE ARE, I'LL BE DONE. CALL NO ONE HAPPY UNTIL THEY'RE DEAD IS AN OLD SAYING. WORTH REPEATING.

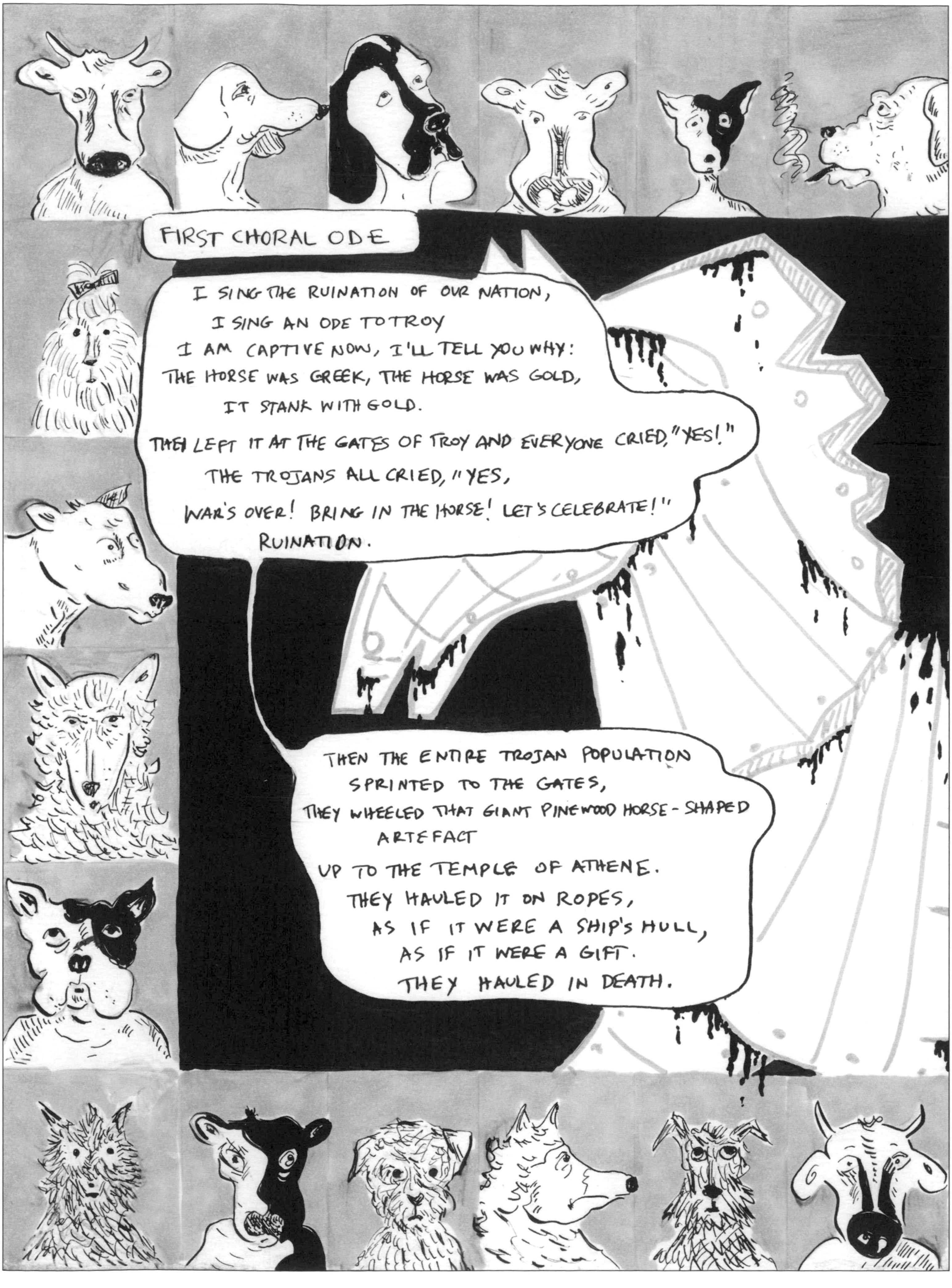

FIRST CHORAL ODE
I SING THE RUINATION OF OUR NATION, I SING AN ODE TO TROY I AM CAPTIVE NOW, I'LL TELL YOU WHY: THE HORSE WAS GREEK, THE HORSE WAS GOLD, IT STANK WITH GOLD. THEY LEFT IT AT THE GATES OF TROY AND EVERYONE CRIED, "YES!" THE TROJANS ALL CRIED, "YES, WAR'S OVER! BRING IN THE HORSE! LET'S CELEBRATE!" RUINATION.
THEN THE ENTIRE TROJAN POPULATION SPRINTED TO THE GATES, THEY WHEELED THAT GIANT PINEWOOD HORSE-SHAPED ARTEFACT UP TO THE TEMPLE OF ATHENE. THEY HAULED IT ON ROPES, AS IF IT WERE A SHIP'S HULL, AS IF IT WERE A GIFT. THEY HAULED IN DEATH.

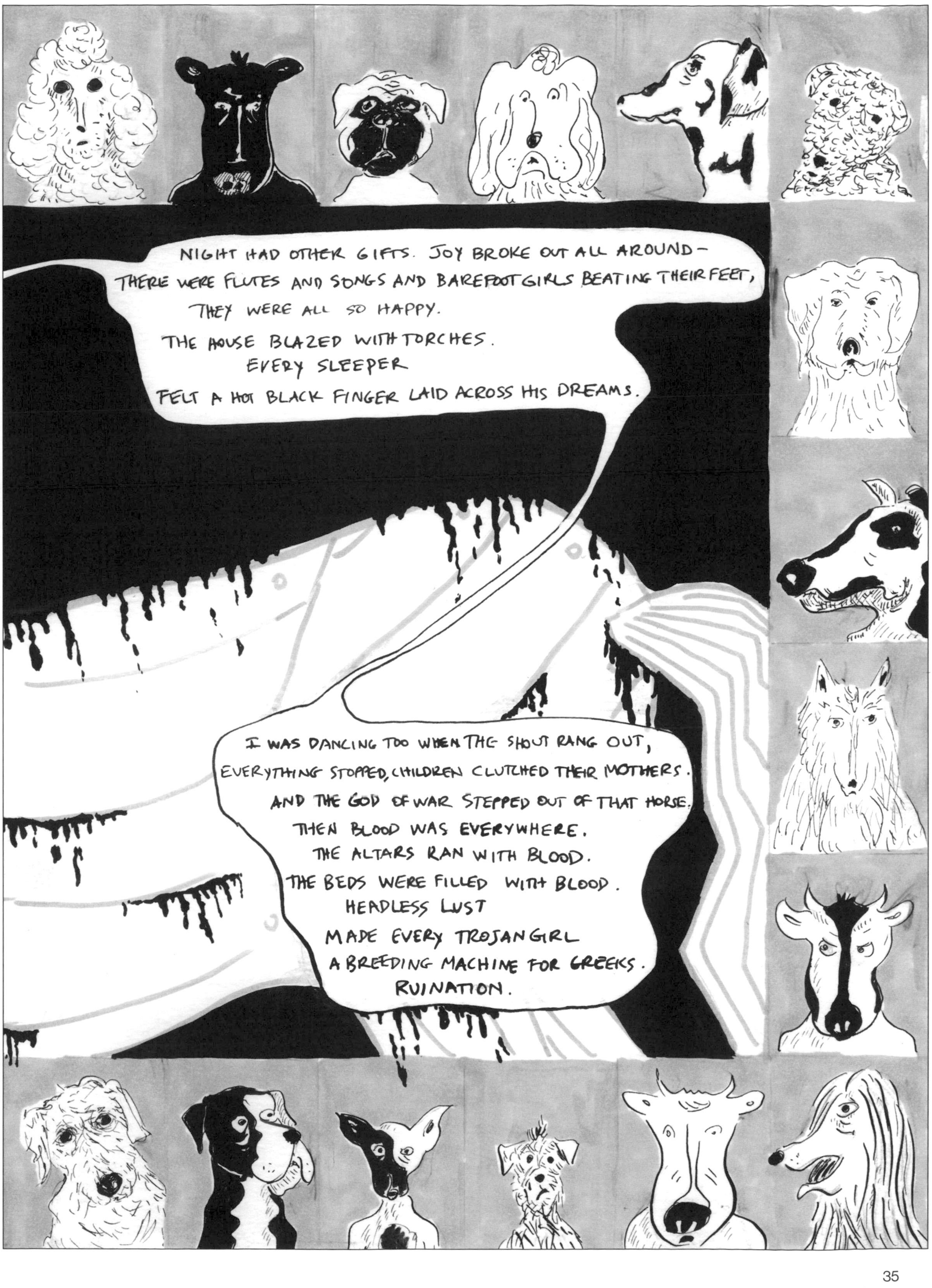
NIGHT HAD OTHER GIFTS. JOY BROKE OUT ALL AROUND—
THERE WERE FLUTES AND SONGS AND BAREFOOT GIRLS BEATING THEIR FEET,
THEY WERE ALL SO HAPPY.
THE HOUSE BLAZED WITH TORCHES.
EVERY SLEEPER
FELT A HOT BLACK FINGER LAID ACROSS HIS DREAMS.
I WAS DANCING TOO WHEN THE SHOUT RANG OUT,
EVERYTHING STOPPED, CHILDREN CLUTCHED THEIR MOTHERS.
AND THE GOD OF WAR STEPPED OUT OF THAT HORSE.
THEN BLOOD WAS EVERYWHERE.
THE ALTARS RAN WITH BLOOD.
THE BEDS WERE FILLED WITH BLOOD.
HEADLESS LUST
MADE EVERY TROJAN GIRL
A BREEDING MACHINE FOR GREEKS.
RUINATION.

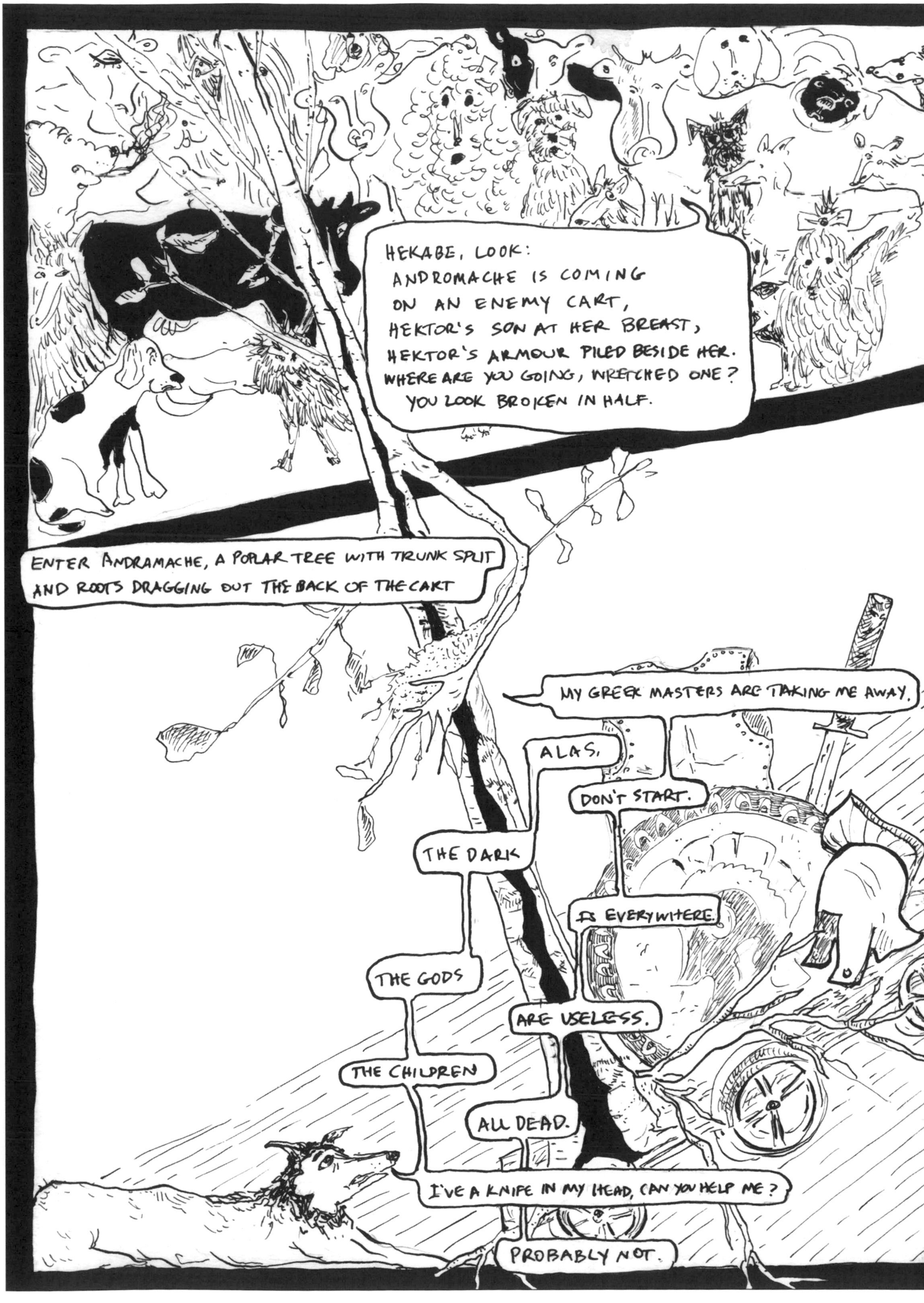
HEKABE, LOOK:
ANDROMACHE IS COMING
ON AN ENEMY CART,
HEKTOR'S SON AT HER BREAST,
HEKTOR'S ARMOUR PILED BESIDE HER.
WHERE ARE YOU GOING, WRETCHED ONE?
YOU LOOK BROKEN IN HALF.
ENTER ANDRAMACHE, A POPLAR TREE WITH TRUNK SPLIT AND ROOTS DRAGGING OUT THE BACK OF THE CART
MY GREEK MASTERS ARE TAKING ME AWAY.
ALAS,
DON'T START.
THE DARK
IS EVERYWHERE.
THE GODS
ARE USELESS.
THE CHILDREN
ALL DEAD.
I'VE A KNIFE IN MY HEAD, CAN YOU HELP ME?
PROBABLY NOT.

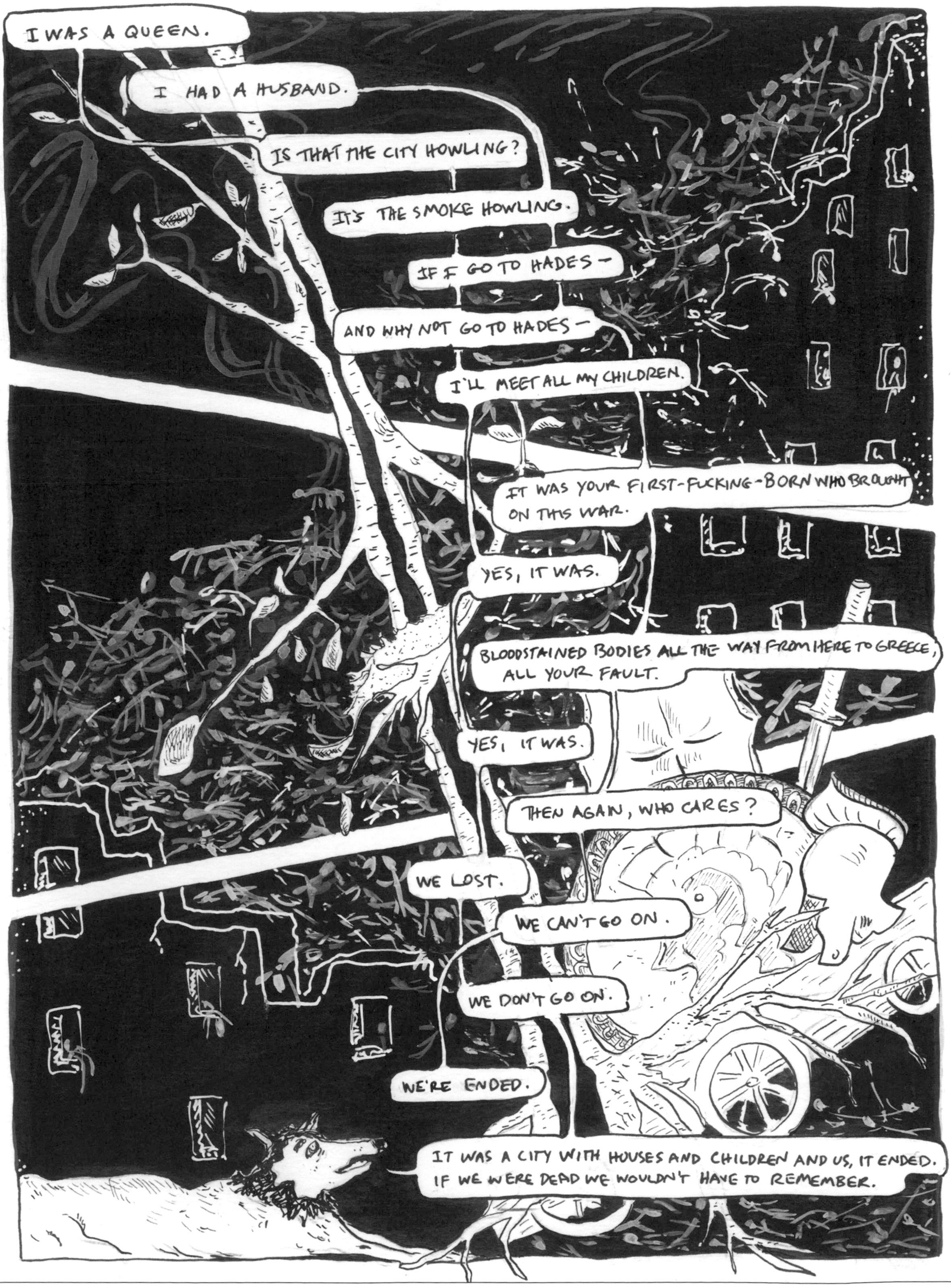
I WAS A QUEEN.
I HAD A HUSBAND.
IS THAT THE CITY HOWLING?
IT'S THE SMOKE HOWLING.
IF I GO TO HADES—
AND WHY NOT GO TO HADES—
I'LL MEET ALL MY CHILDREN.
IT WAS YOUR FIRST-FUCKING-BORN WHO BROUGHT ON THIS WAR.
YES, IT WAS.
BLOODSTAINED BODIES ALL THE WAY FROM HERE TO GREECE, ALL YOUR FAULT.
YES, IT WAS.
THEN AGAIN, WHO CARES?
WE LOST.
WE CAN'T GO ON.
WE DON'T GO ON.
WE'RE ENDED.
IT WAS A CITY WITH HOUSES AND CHILDREN AND US, IT ENDED. IF WE WERE DEAD WE WOULDN'T HAVE TO REMEMBER.

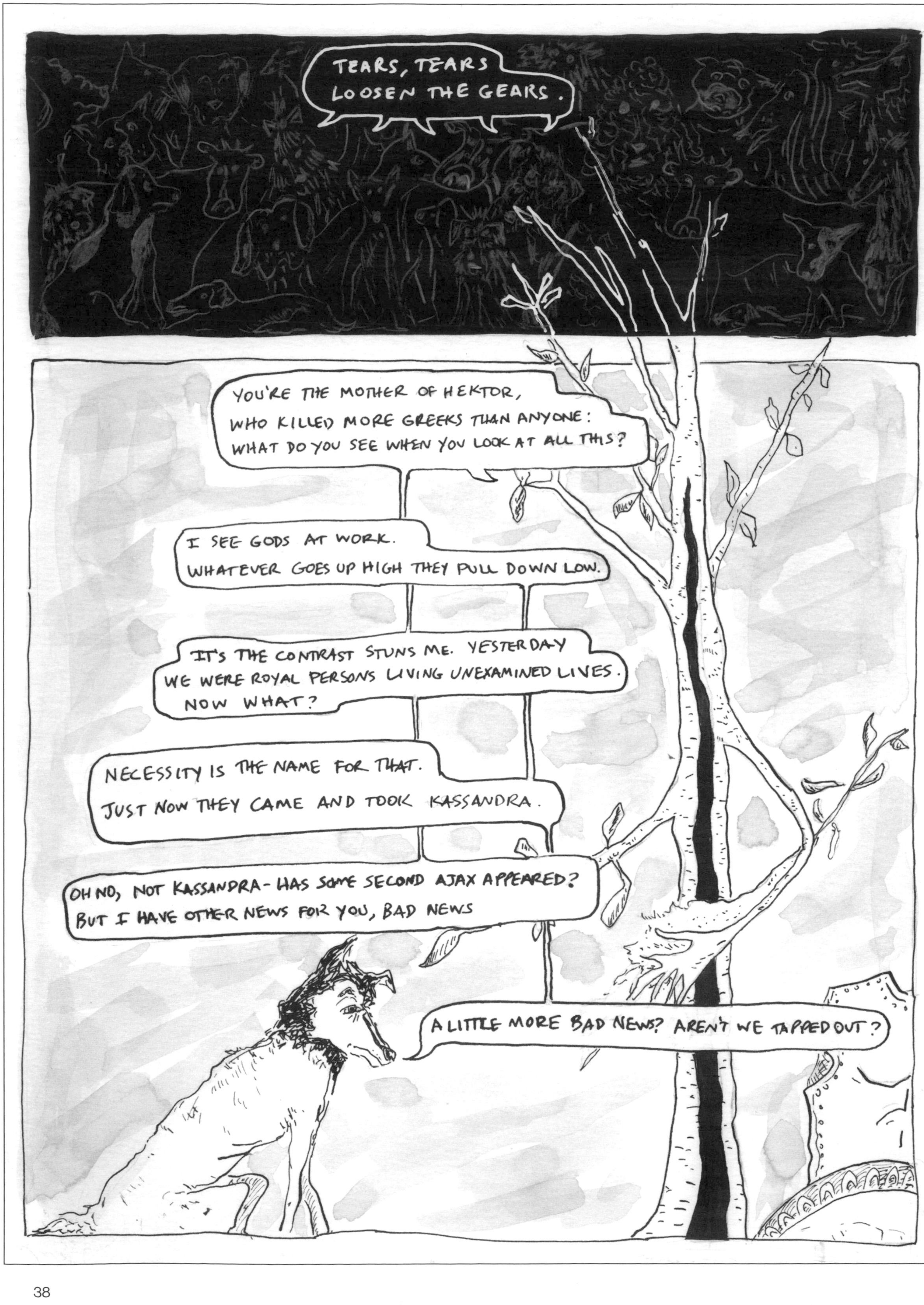
TEARS, TEARS LOOSEN THE GEARS.
YOU'RE THE MOTHER OF HEKTOR, WHO KILLED MORE GREEKS THAN ANYONE: WHAT DO YOU SEE WHEN YOU LOOK AT ALL THIS?
I SEE GODS AT WORK. WHATEVER GOES UP HIGH THEY PULL DOWN LOW.
IT'S THE CONTRAST STUNS ME. YESTERDAY WE WERE ROYAL PERSONS LIVING UNEXAMINED LIVES. NOW WHAT?
NECESSITY IS THE NAME FOR THAT. JUST NOW THEY CAME AND TOOK KASSANDRA.
OH NO, NOT KASSANDRA- HAS SOME SECOND AJAX APPEARED? BUT I HAVE OTHER NEWS FOR YOU, BAD NEWS
A LITTLE MORE BAD NEWS? AREN'T WE TAPPED OUT?

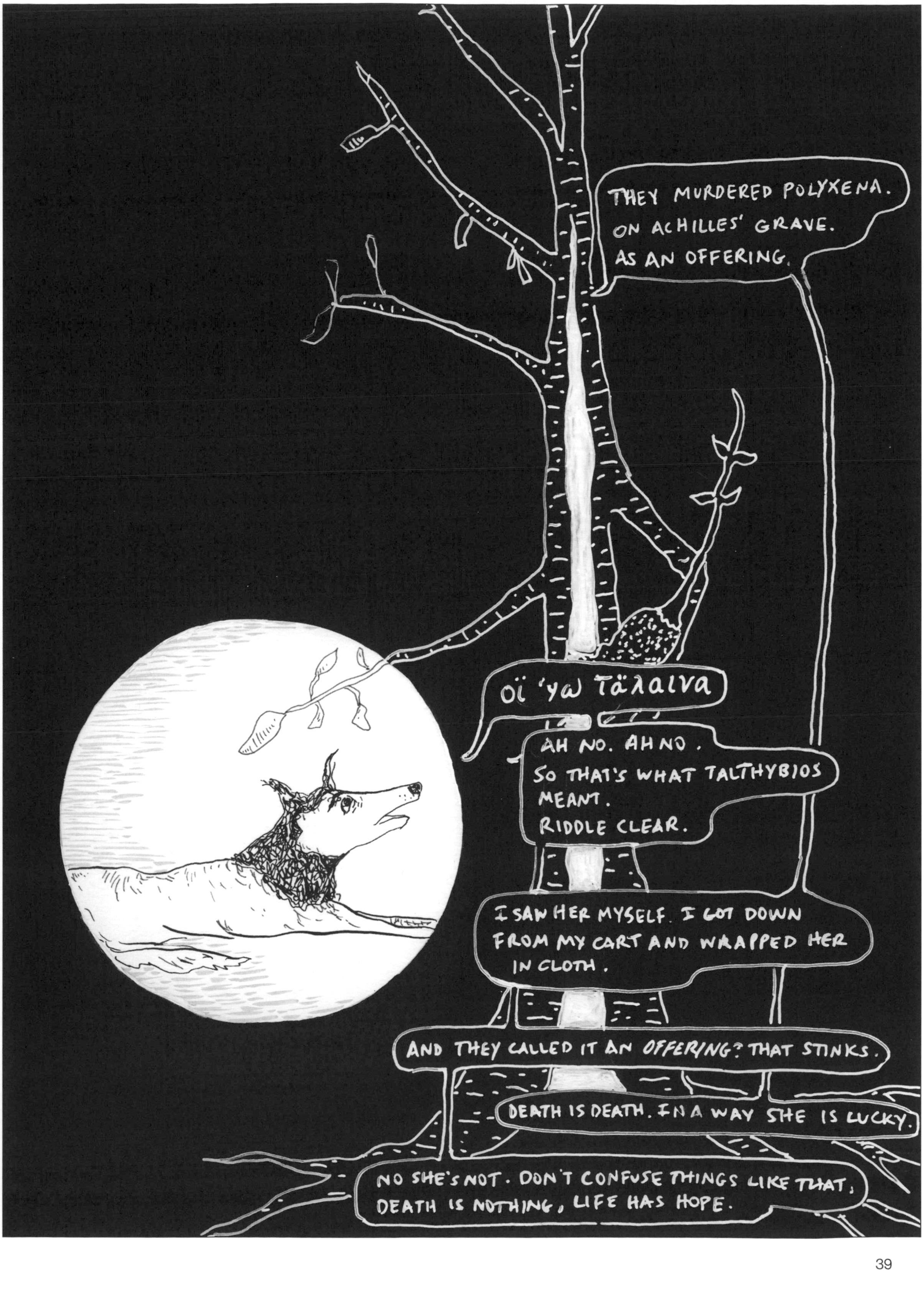
THEY MURDERED POLYXENA. ON ACHILLES' GRAVE. AS AN OFFERING.
οἴ 'γω τάλαινα
AH NO. AH NO. SO THAT'S WHAT TALTHYBIOS MEANT. RIDDLE CLEAR.
I SAW HER MYSELF. I GOT DOWN FROM MY CART AND WRAPPED HER IN CLOTH.
AND THEY CALLED IT AN *OFFERING*? THAT STINKS.
DEATH IS DEATH. IN A WAY SHE IS LUCKY.
NO SHE'S NOT. DON'T CONFUSE THINGS LIKE THAT; DEATH IS NOTHING, LIFE HAS HOPE.

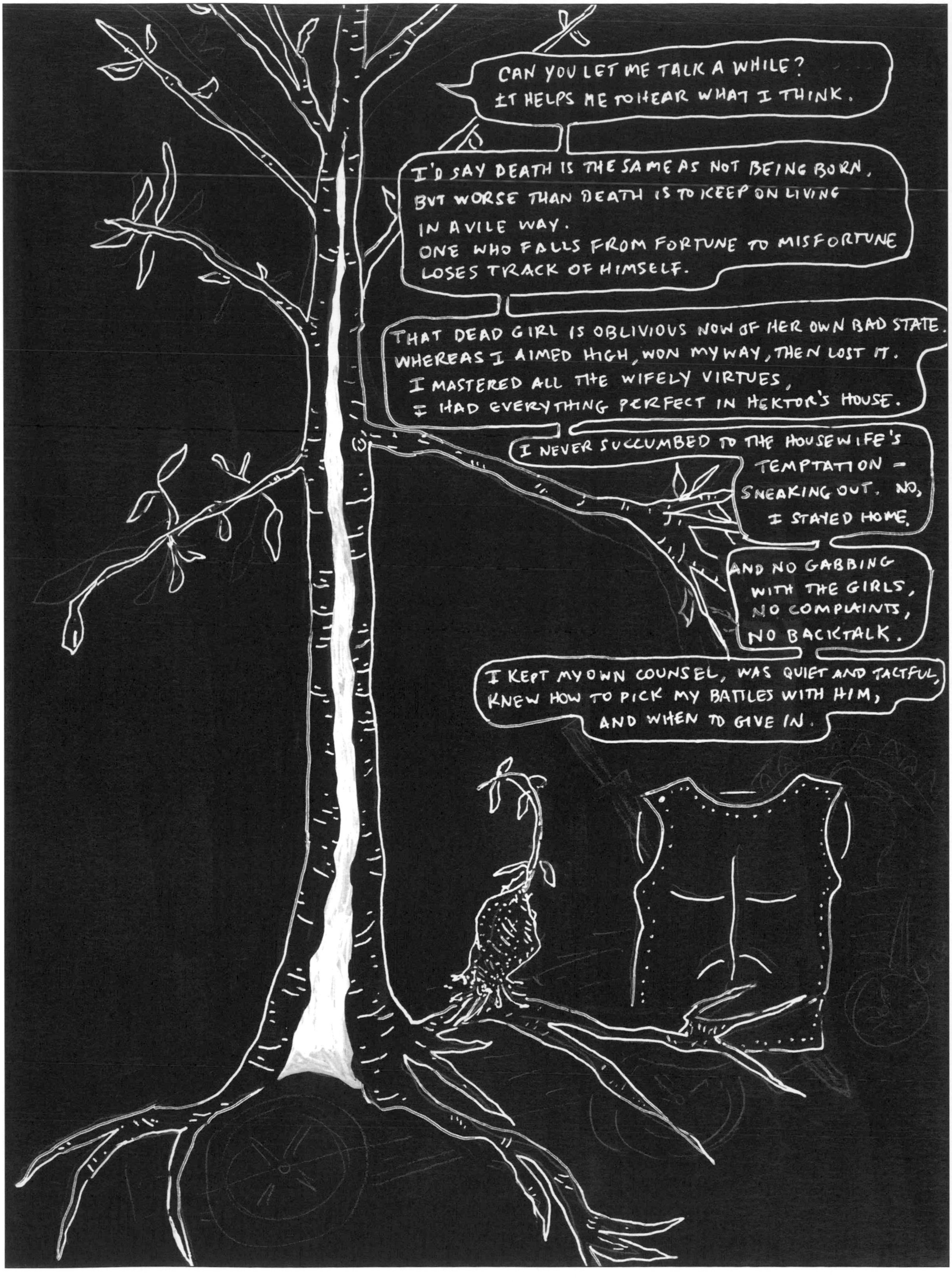

CAN YOU LET ME TALK A WHILE? IT HELPS ME TO HEAR WHAT I THINK.
I'D SAY DEATH IS THE SAME AS NOT BEING BORN, BUT WORSE THAN DEATH IS TO KEEP ON LIVING IN A VILE WAY. ONE WHO FALLS FROM FORTUNE TO MISFORTUNE LOSES TRACK OF HIMSELF.
THAT DEAD GIRL IS OBLIVIOUS NOW OF HER OWN BAD STATE. WHEREAS I AIMED HIGH, WON MY WAY, THEN LOST IT. I MASTERED ALL THE WIFELY VIRTUES, I HAD EVERYTHING PERFECT IN HEKTOR'S HOUSE.
I NEVER SUCCUMBED TO THE HOUSEWIFE'S TEMPTATION – SNEAKING OUT. NO, I STAYED HOME.
AND NO GABBING WITH THE GIRLS, NO COMPLAINTS, NO BACKTALK.
I KEPT MY OWN COUNSEL, WAS QUIET AND TACTFUL, KNEW HOW TO PICK MY BATTLES WITH HIM, AND WHEN TO GIVE IN.

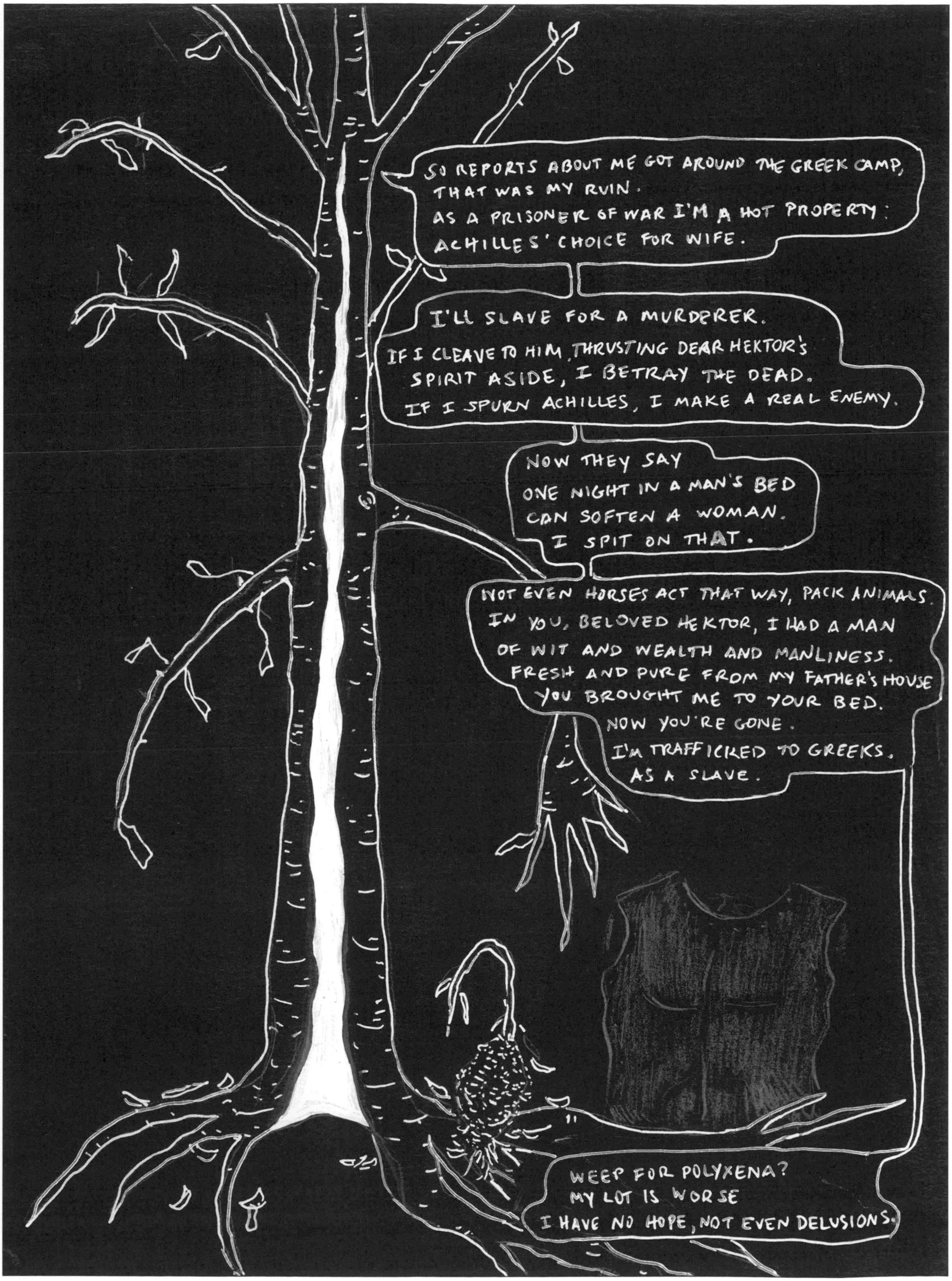
SO REPORTS ABOUT ME GOT AROUND THE GREEK CAMP, THAT WAS MY RUIN. AS A PRISONER OF WAR I'M A HOT PROPERTY: ACHILLES' CHOICE FOR WIFE.
I'LL SLAVE FOR A MURDERER. IF I CLEAVE TO HIM, THRUSTING DEAR HEKTOR'S SPIRIT ASIDE, I BETRAY THE DEAD. IF I SPURN ACHILLES, I MAKE A REAL ENEMY.
NOW THEY SAY ONE NIGHT IN A MAN'S BED CAN SOFTEN A WOMAN. I SPIT ON THAT.
NOT EVEN HORSES ACT THAT WAY, PACK ANIMALS. IN YOU, BELOVED HEKTOR, I HAD A MAN OF WIT AND WEALTH AND MANLINESS. FRESH AND PURE FROM MY FATHER'S HOUSE YOU BROUGHT ME TO YOUR BED. NOW YOU'RE GONE. I'M TRAFFICKED TO GREEKS. AS A SLAVE.
WEEP FOR POLYXENA? MY LOT IS WORSE I HAVE NO HOPE, NOT EVEN DELUSIONS.

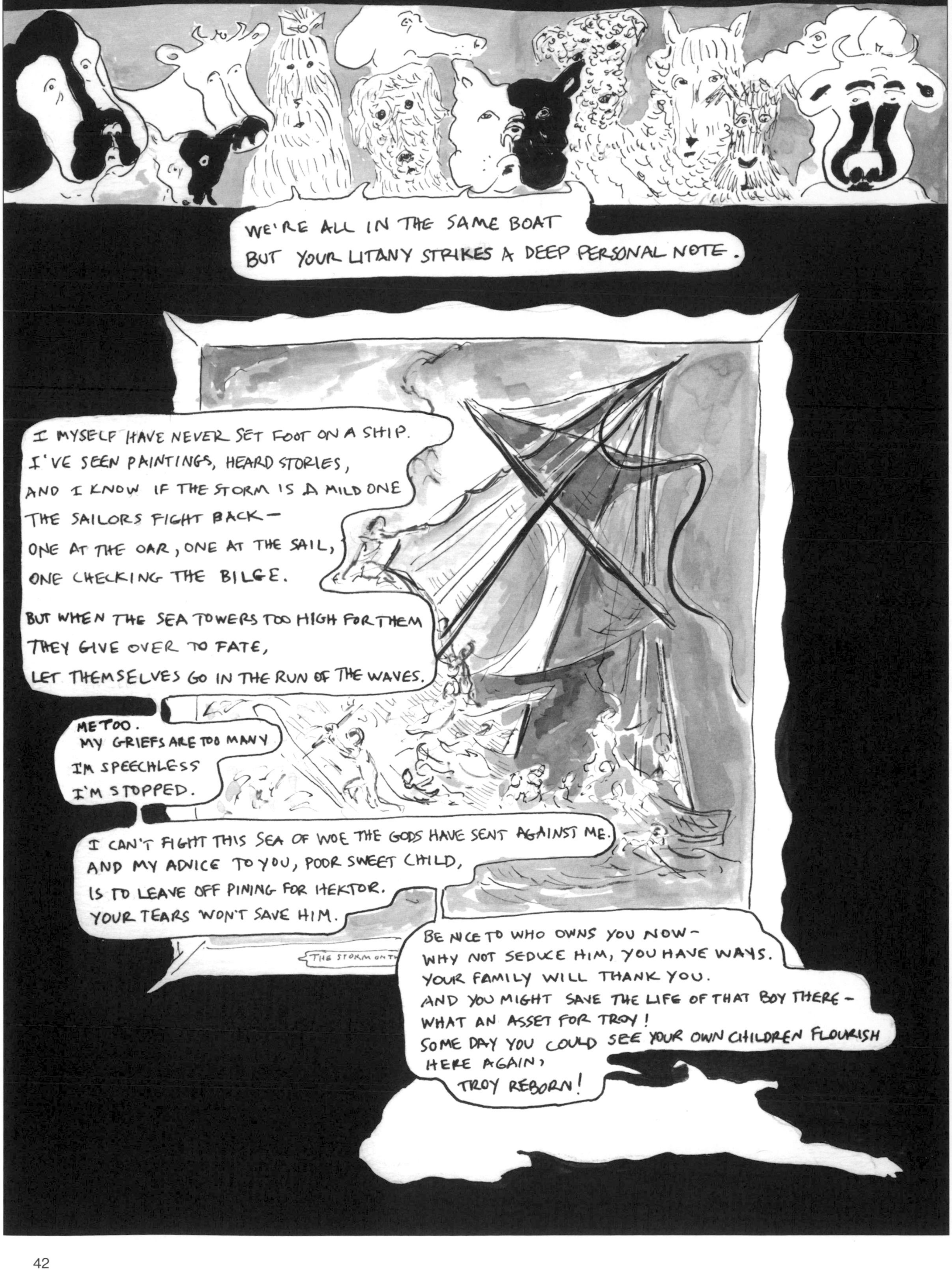
WE'RE ALL IN THE SAME BOAT
BUT YOUR LITANY STRIKES A DEEP PERSONAL NOTE.
I MYSELF HAVE NEVER SET FOOT ON A SHIP. I'VE SEEN PAINTINGS, HEARD STORIES, AND I KNOW IF THE STORM IS A MILD ONE THE SAILORS FIGHT BACK— ONE AT THE OAR, ONE AT THE SAIL, ONE CHECKING THE BILGE. BUT WHEN THE SEA TOWERS TOO HIGH FOR THEM THEY GIVE OVER TO FATE, LET THEMSELVES GO IN THE RUN OF THE WAVES.
ME TOO. MY GRIEFS ARE TOO MANY I'M SPEECHLESS I'M STOPPED.
I CAN'T FIGHT THIS SEA OF WOE THE GODS HAVE SENT AGAINST ME. AND MY ADVICE TO YOU, POOR SWEET CHILD, IS TO LEAVE OFF PINING FOR HEKTOR. YOUR TEARS WON'T SAVE HIM.
BE NICE TO WHO OWNS YOU NOW— WHY NOT SEDUCE HIM, YOU HAVE WAYS. YOUR FAMILY WILL THANK YOU. AND YOU MIGHT SAVE THE LIFE OF THAT BOY THERE— WHAT AN ASSET FOR TROY! SOME DAY YOU COULD SEE YOUR OWN CHILDREN FLOURISH HERE AGAIN, TROY REBORN!

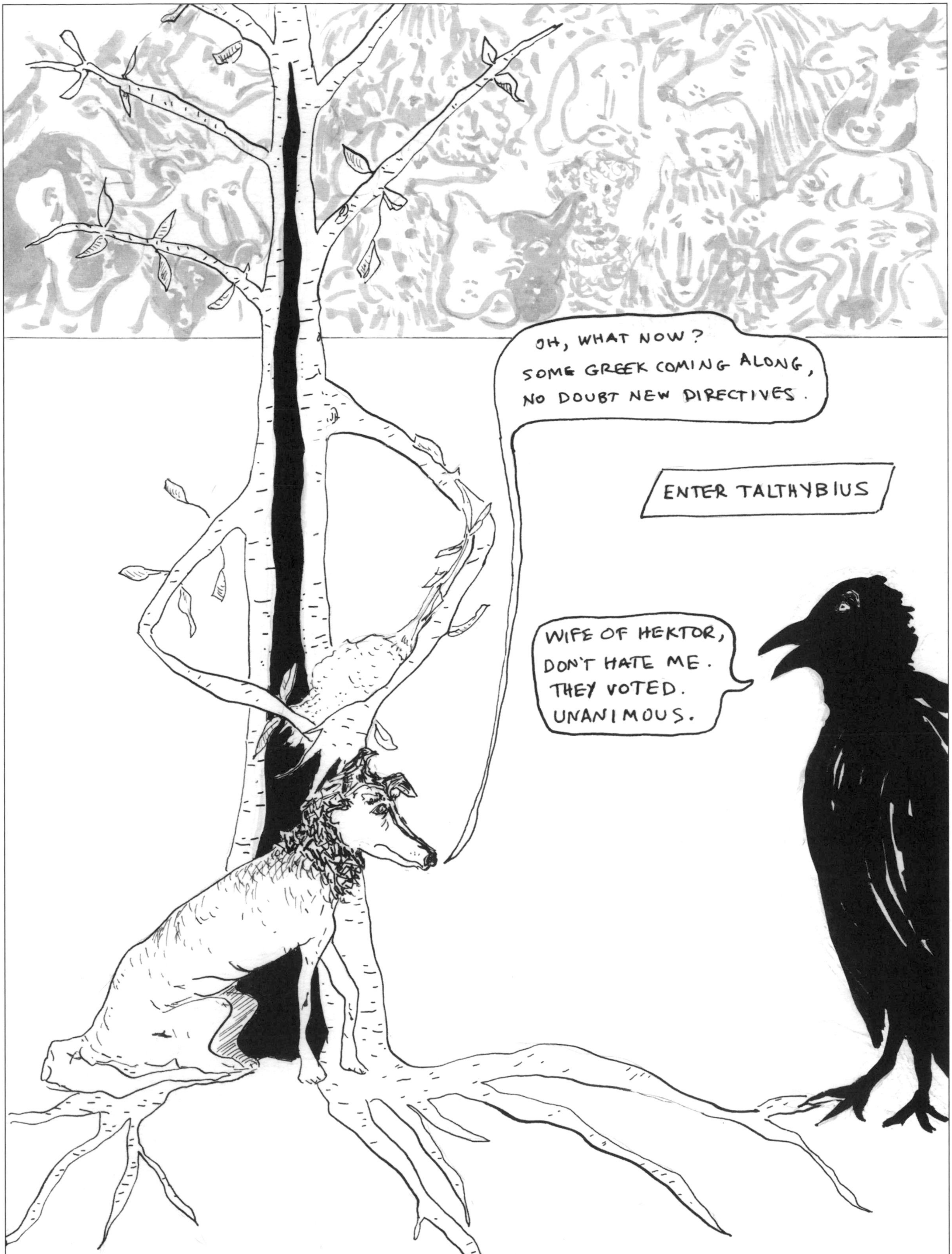
OH, WHAT NOW? SOME GREEK COMING ALONG, NO DOUBT NEW DIRECTIVES.
ENTER TALTHYBIUS
WIFE OF HEKTOR, DON'T HATE ME. THEY VOTED. UNANIMOUS.

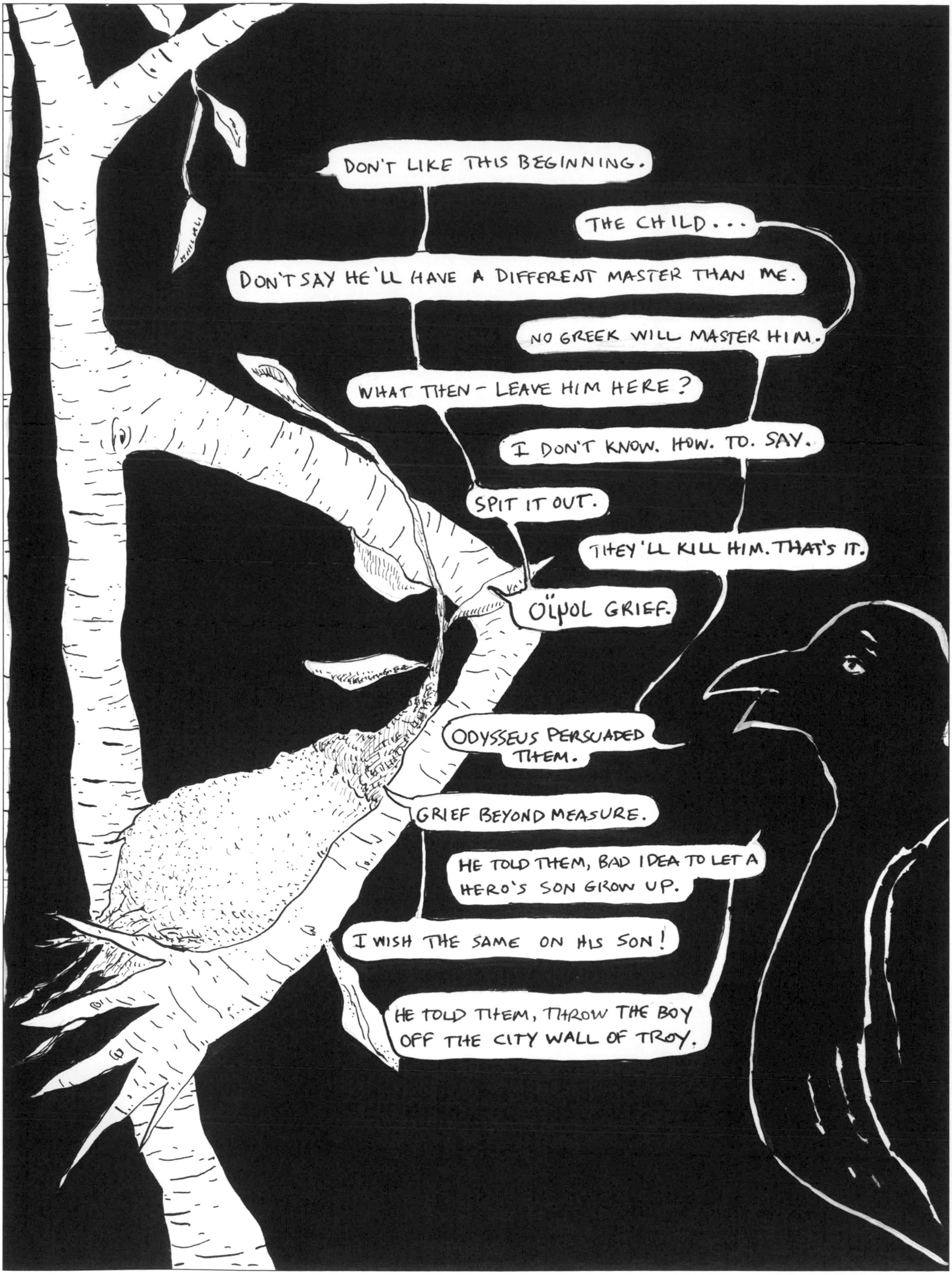
DON'T LIKE THIS BEGINNING.
THE CHILD...
DON'T SAY HE'LL HAVE A DIFFERENT MASTER THAN ME.
NO GREEK WILL MASTER HIM.
WHAT THEN - LEAVE HIM HERE?
I DON'T KNOW. HOW. TO. SAY.
SPIT IT OUT.
THEY'LL KILL HIM. THAT'S IT.
OÏμOL GRIEF.
ODYSSEUS PERSUADED THEM.
GRIEF BEYOND MEASURE.
HE TOLD THEM, BAD IDEA TO LET A HERO'S SON GROW UP.
I WISH THE SAME ON HIS SON!
HE TOLD THEM, THROW THE BOY OFF THE CITY WALL OF TROY.

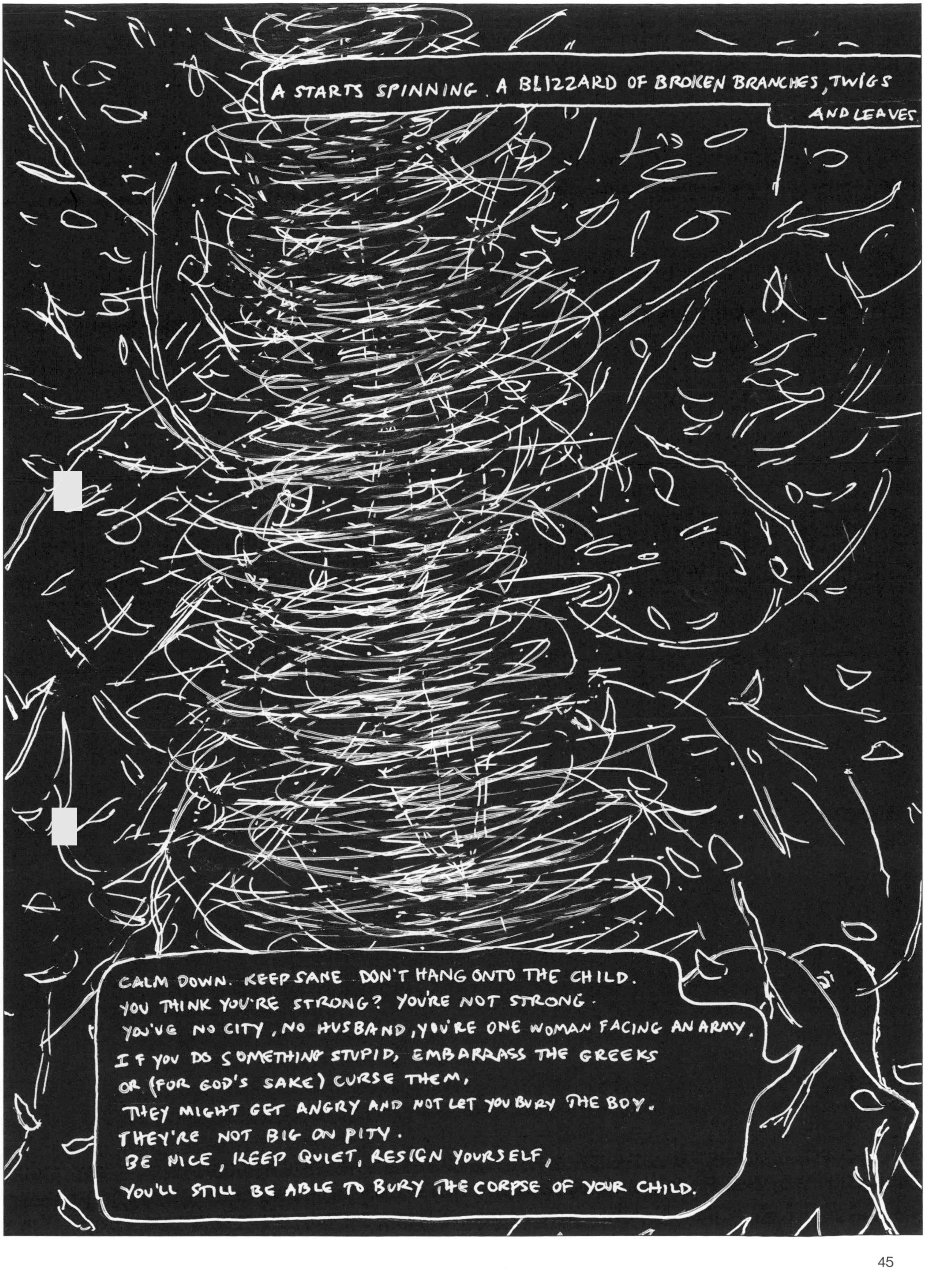
A STARTS SPINNING. A BLIZZARD OF BROKEN BRANCHES, TWIGS AND LEAVES.
CALM DOWN. KEEP SANE. DON'T HANG ONTO THE CHILD.
YOU THINK YOU'RE STRONG? YOU'RE NOT STRONG.
YOU'VE NO CITY, NO HUSBAND, YOU'RE ONE WOMAN FACING AN ARMY.
IF YOU DO SOMETHING STUPID, EMBARRASS THE GREEKS
OR (FOR GOD'S SAKE) CURSE THEM,
THEY MIGHT GET ANGRY AND NOT LET YOU BURY THE BOY.
THEY'RE NOT BIG ON PITY.
BE NICE, KEEP QUIET, RESIGN YOURSELF,
YOU'LL STILL BE ABLE TO BURY THE CORPSE OF YOUR CHILD.

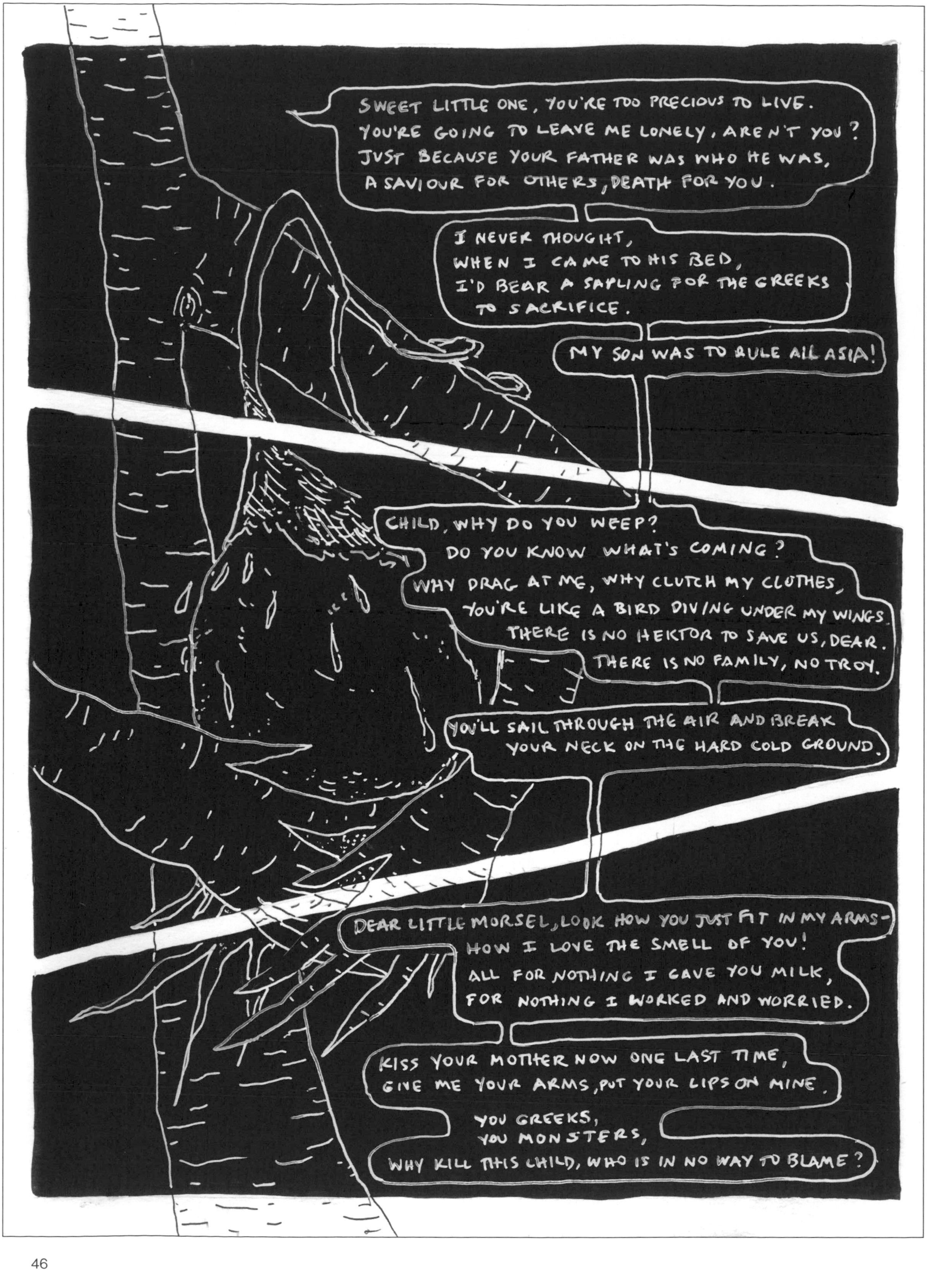
SWEET LITTLE ONE, YOU'RE TOO PRECIOUS TO LIVE. YOU'RE GOING TO LEAVE ME LONELY, AREN'T YOU? JUST BECAUSE YOUR FATHER WAS WHO HE WAS, A SAVIOUR FOR OTHERS, DEATH FOR YOU.
I NEVER THOUGHT, WHEN I CAME TO HIS BED, I'D BEAR A SAPLING FOR THE GREEKS TO SACRIFICE.
MY SON WAS TO RULE ALL ASIA!
CHILD, WHY DO YOU WEEP? DO YOU KNOW WHAT'S COMING? WHY DRAG AT ME, WHY CLUTCH MY CLOTHES, YOU'RE LIKE A BIRD DIVING UNDER MY WINGS. THERE IS NO HEKTOR TO SAVE US, DEAR. THERE IS NO FAMILY, NO TROY.
YOU'LL SAIL THROUGH THE AIR AND BREAK YOUR NECK ON THE HARD COLD GROUND.
DEAR LITTLE MORSEL, LOOK HOW YOU JUST FIT IN MY ARMS- HOW I LOVE THE SMELL OF YOU! ALL FOR NOTHING I GAVE YOU MILK, FOR NOTHING I WORKED AND WORRIED.
KISS YOUR MOTHER NOW ONE LAST TIME, GIVE ME YOUR ARMS, PUT YOUR LIPS ON MINE.
YOU GREEKS, YOU MONSTERS, WHY KILL THIS CHILD, WHO IS IN NO WAY TO BLAME?

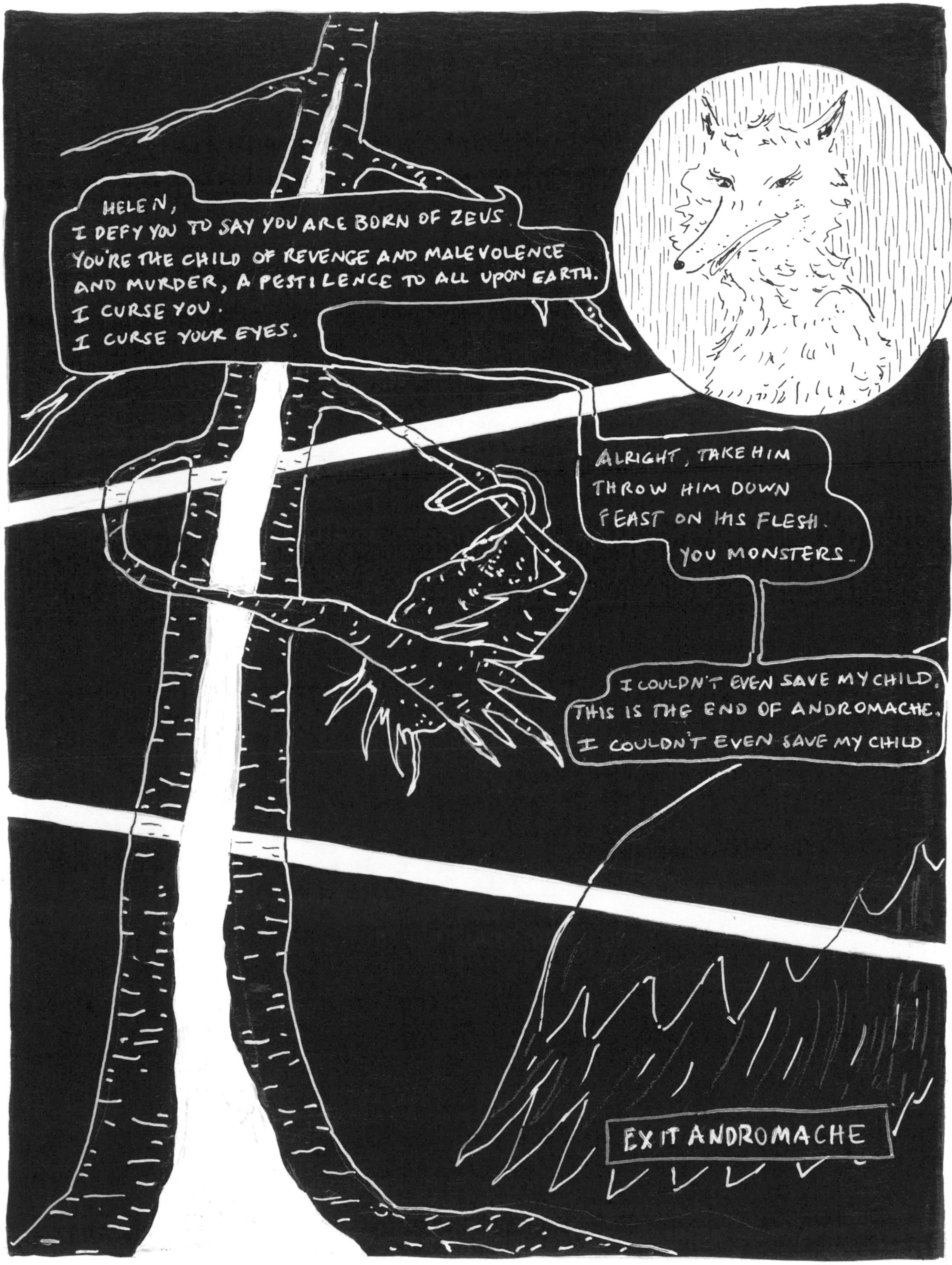
HELEN,
I DEFY YOU TO SAY YOU ARE BORN OF ZEUS.
YOU'RE THE CHILD OF REVENGE AND MALEVOLENCE
AND MURDER, A PESTILENCE TO ALL UPON EARTH.
I CURSE YOU.
I CURSE YOUR EYES.
ALRIGHT, TAKE HIM
THROW HIM DOWN
FEAST ON HIS FLESH.
YOU MONSTERS.
I COULDN'T EVEN SAVE MY CHILD.
THIS IS THE END OF ANDROMACHE.
I COULDN'T EVEN SAVE MY CHILD.
EXIT ANDROMACHE

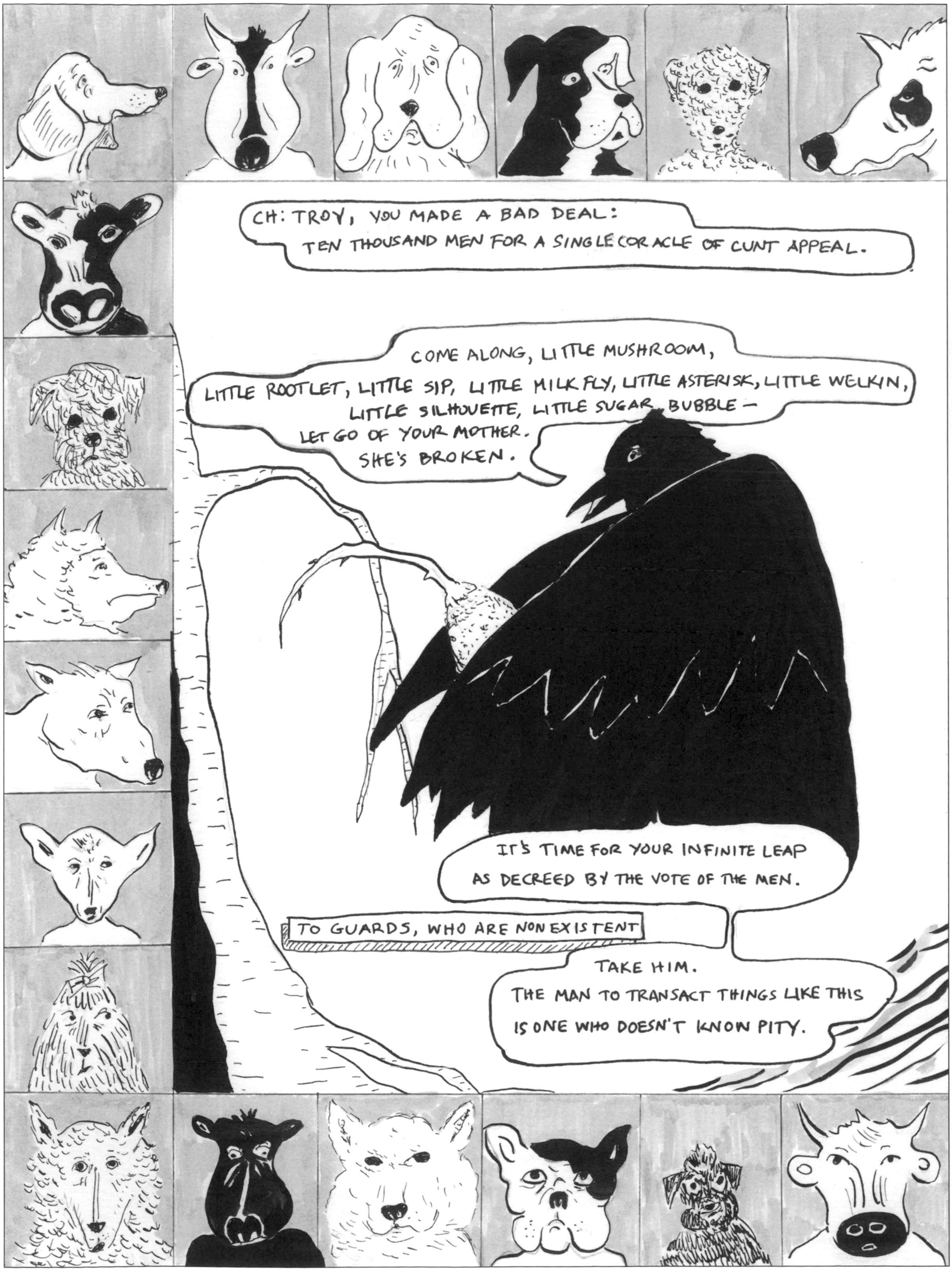
CH: TROY, YOU MADE A BAD DEAL: TEN THOUSAND MEN FOR A SINGLE CORACLE OF CUNT APPEAL.
COME ALONG, LITTLE MUSHROOM, LITTLE ROOTLET, LITTLE SIP, LITTLE MILK FLY, LITTLE ASTERISK, LITTLE WELKIN, LITTLE SILHOUETTE, LITTLE SUGAR BUBBLE — LET GO OF YOUR MOTHER. SHE'S BROKEN.
IT'S TIME FOR YOUR INFINITE LEAP AS DECREED BY THE VOTE OF THE MEN.
TO GUARDS, WHO ARE NONEXISTENT
TAKE HIM. THE MAN TO TRANSACT THINGS LIKE THIS IS ONE WHO DOESN'T KNOW PITY.

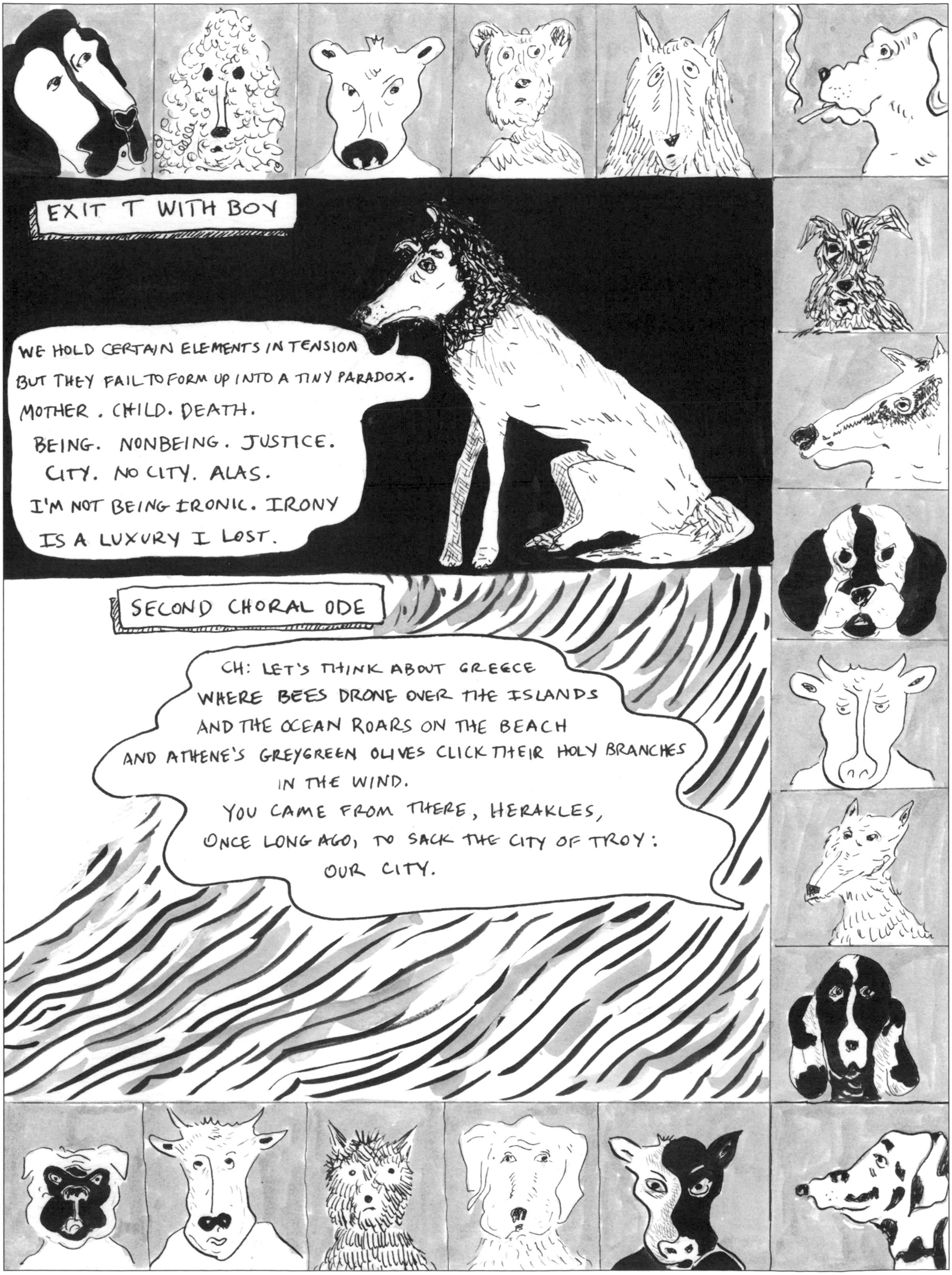
EXIT T WITH BOY
WE HOLD CERTAIN ELEMENTS IN TENSION BUT THEY FAIL TO FORM UP INTO A TINY PARADOX. MOTHER. CHILD. DEATH. BEING. NONBEING. JUSTICE. CITY. NO CITY. ALAS. I'M NOT BEING IRONIC. IRONY IS A LUXURY I LOST.
SECOND CHORAL ODE
CH: LET'S THINK ABOUT GREECE WHERE BEES DRONE OVER THE ISLANDS AND THE OCEAN ROARS ON THE BEACH AND ATHENE'S GREYGREEN OLIVES CLICK THEIR HOLY BRANCHES IN THE WIND. YOU CAME FROM THERE, HERAKLES, ONCE LONG AGO, TO SACK THE CITY OF TROY: OUR CITY.

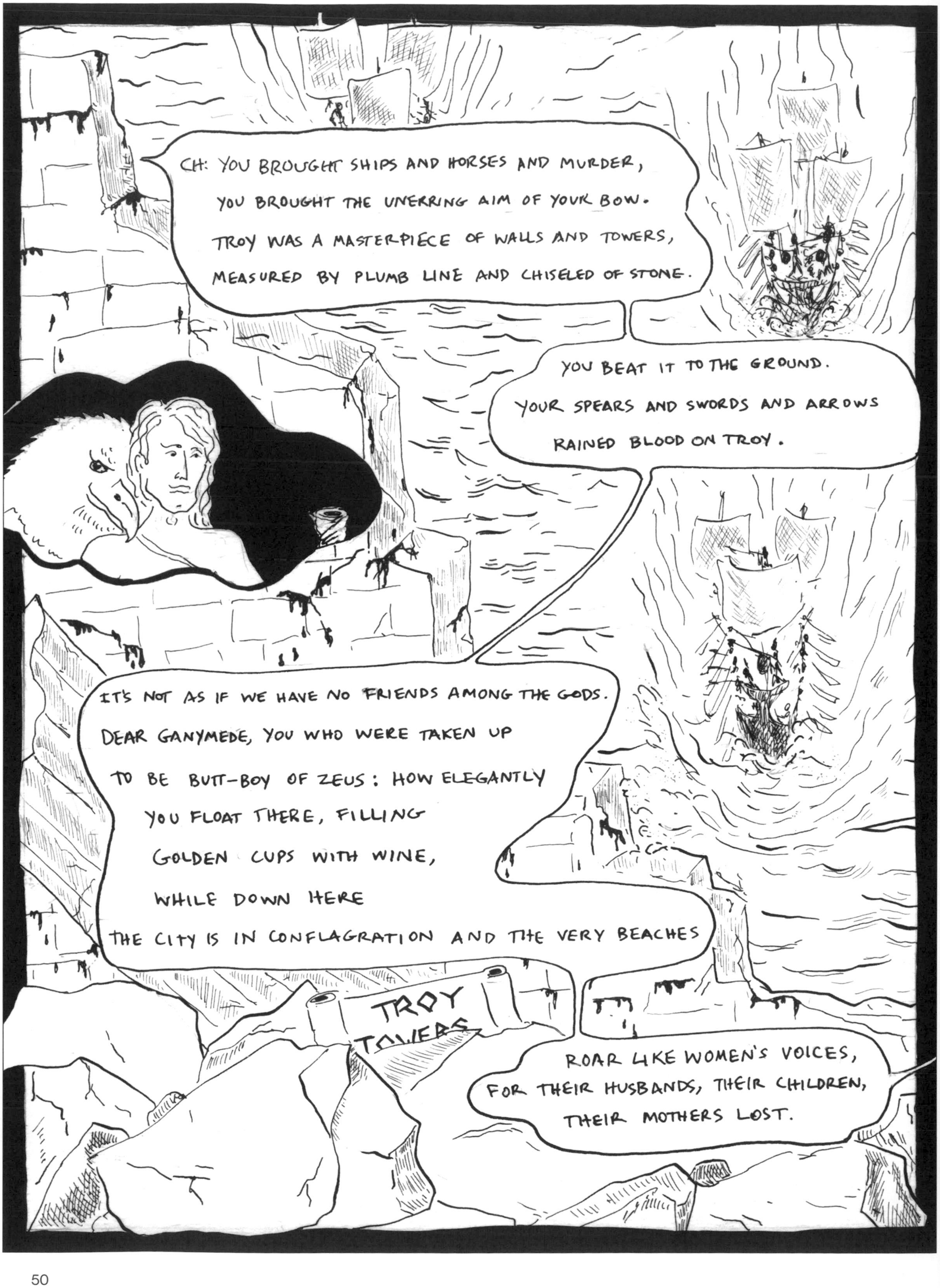
CH: YOU BROUGHT SHIPS AND HORSES AND MURDER, YOU BROUGHT THE UNERRING AIM OF YOUR BOW. TROY WAS A MASTERPIECE OF WALLS AND TOWERS, MEASURED BY PLUMB LINE AND CHISELED OF STONE.
YOU BEAT IT TO THE GROUND. YOUR SPEARS AND SWORDS AND ARROWS RAINED BLOOD ON TROY.
IT'S NOT AS IF WE HAVE NO FRIENDS AMONG THE GODS. DEAR GANYMEDE, YOU WHO WERE TAKEN UP TO BE BUTT-BOY OF ZEUS: HOW ELEGANTLY YOU FLOAT THERE, FILLING GOLDEN CUPS WITH WINE, WHILE DOWN HERE THE CITY IS IN CONFLAGRATION AND THE VERY BEACHES
TROY
ROAR LIKE WOMEN'S VOICES, FOR THEIR HUSBANDS, THEIR CHILDREN, THEIR MOTHERS LOST.

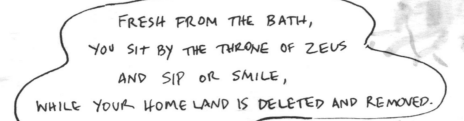

FRESH FROM THE BATH,
YOU SIT BY THE THRONE OF ZEUS
AND SIP OR SMILE,
WHILE YOUR HOME LAND IS DELETED AND REMOVED.

EROS, DEAR EROS,
YOU CAME TO TROY AND BROUGHT DESIRE WITH YOU
YOU MADE TROY GREAT BY PIMPING HER TO THE GODS
(NO USE REPROACHING ZEUS WITH THAT).
TITHONOS WAS OUR LAST HOPE.
WHEN THE GODDESS OF DAWN ON HER TRANSPARENT WINGS
CHOSE HIM AS HUSBAND,
WE THOUGHT THINGS WERE GOING TO BE OKAY.
BUT THE GODS'
LOVE
LEFT
TROY.

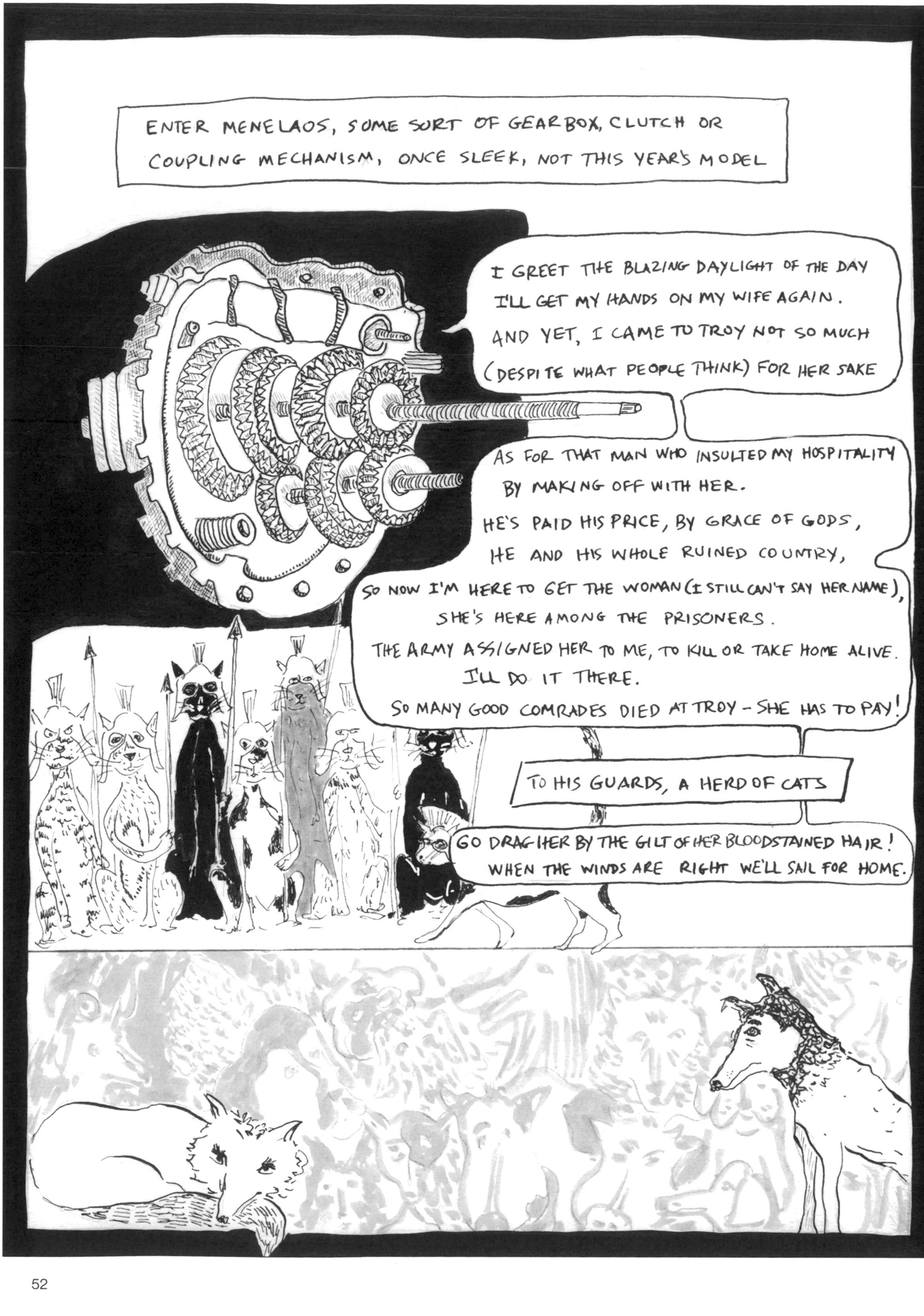
ENTER MENELAOS, SOME SORT OF GEARBOX, CLUTCH OR COUPLING MECHANISM, ONCE SLEEK, NOT THIS YEAR'S MODEL
I GREET THE BLAZING DAYLIGHT OF THE DAY I'LL GET MY HANDS ON MY WIFE AGAIN. AND YET, I CAME TO TROY NOT SO MUCH (DESPITE WHAT PEOPLE THINK) FOR HER SAKE
AS FOR THAT MAN WHO INSULTED MY HOSPITALITY BY MAKING OFF WITH HER. HE'S PAID HIS PRICE, BY GRACE OF GODS, HE AND HIS WHOLE RUINED COUNTRY, SO NOW I'M HERE TO GET THE WOMAN (I STILL CAN'T SAY HER NAME), SHE'S HERE AMONG THE PRISONERS. THE ARMY ASSIGNED HER TO ME, TO KILL OR TAKE HOME ALIVE. I'LL DO IT THERE. SO MANY GOOD COMRADES DIED AT TROY - SHE HAS TO PAY!
TO HIS GUARDS, A HERD OF CATS
GO DRAG HER BY THE GILT OF HER BLOODSTAINED HAIR! WHEN THE WINDS ARE RIGHT WE'LL SAIL FOR HOME.

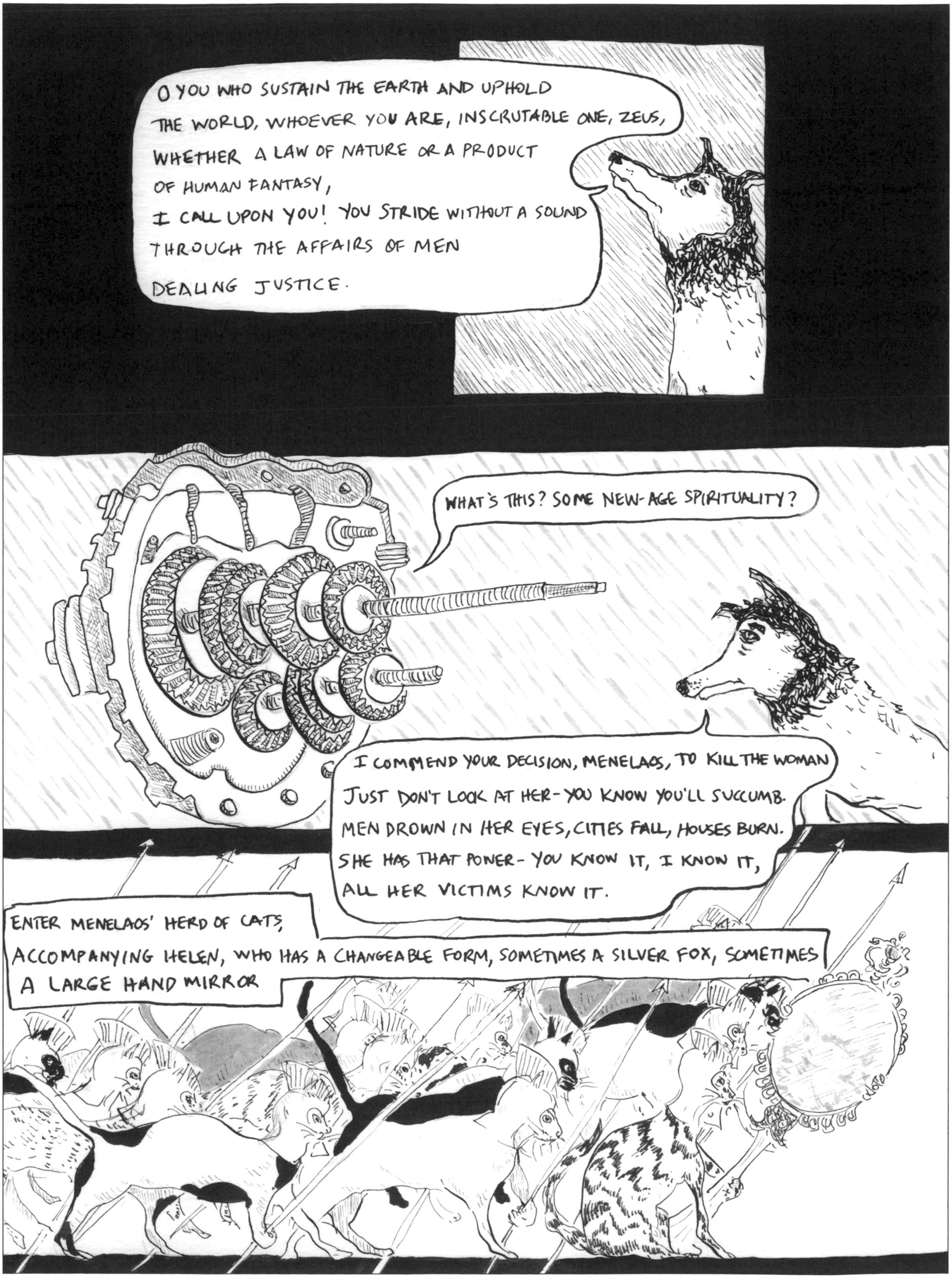
O YOU WHO SUSTAIN THE EARTH AND UPHOLD THE WORLD, WHOEVER YOU ARE, INSCRUTABLE ONE, ZEUS, WHETHER A LAW OF NATURE OR A PRODUCT OF HUMAN FANTASY, I CALL UPON YOU! YOU STRIDE WITHOUT A SOUND THROUGH THE AFFAIRS OF MEN DEALING JUSTICE.
WHAT'S THIS? SOME NEW-AGE SPIRITUALITY?
I COMMEND YOUR DECISION, MENELAOS, TO KILL THE WOMAN JUST DON'T LOOK AT HER- YOU KNOW YOU'LL SUCCUMB. MEN DROWN IN HER EYES, CITIES FALL, HOUSES BURN. SHE HAS THAT POWER- YOU KNOW IT, I KNOW IT, ALL HER VICTIMS KNOW IT.
ENTER MENELAOS' HERD OF CATS,
ACCOMPANYING HELEN, WHO HAS A CHANGEABLE FORM, SOMETIMES A SILVER FOX, SOMETIMES A LARGE HAND MIRROR

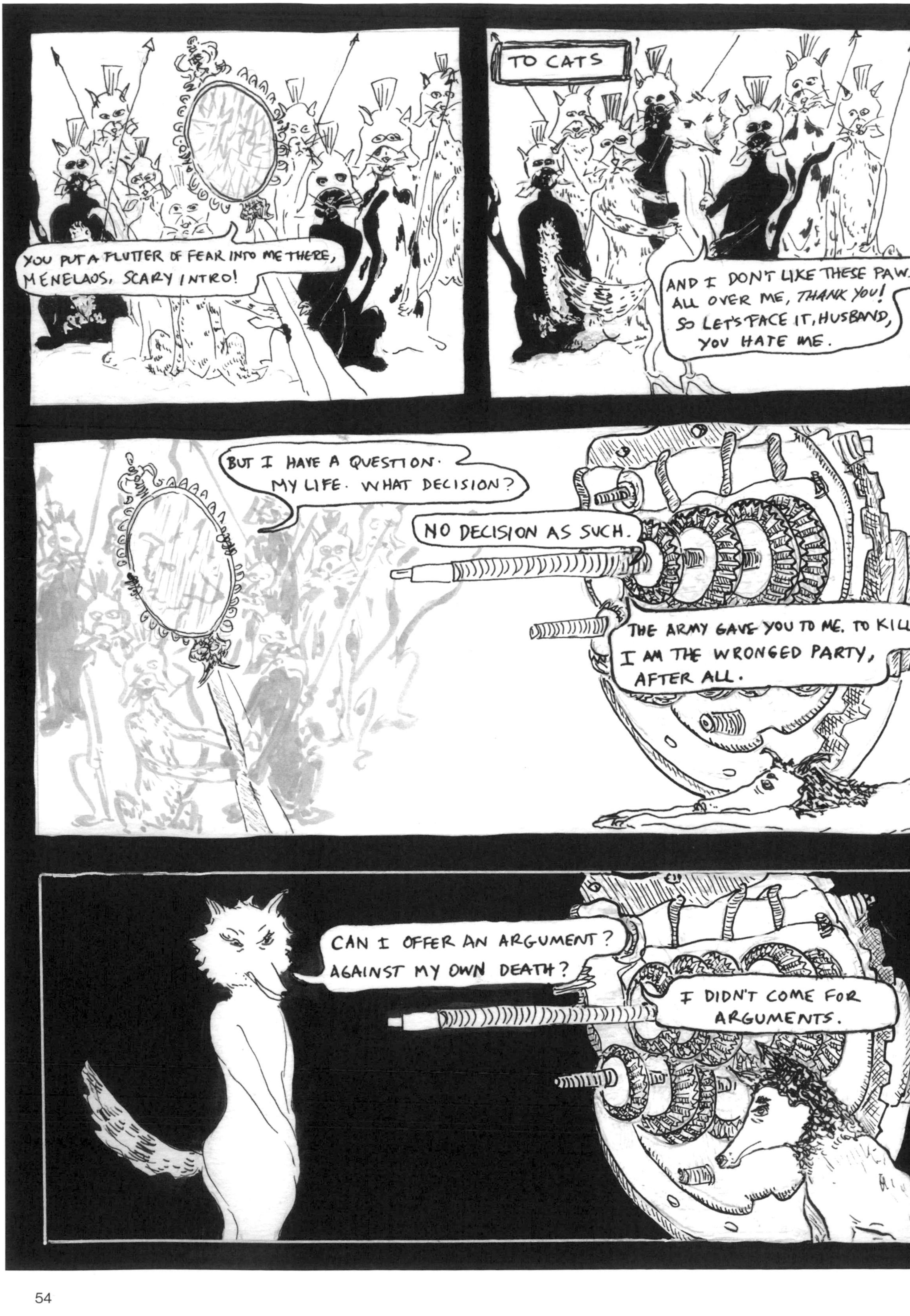
YOU PUT A FLUTTER OF FEAR INTO ME THERE, MENELAOS, SCARY INTRO!
TO CATS
AND I DON'T LIKE THESE PAWS ALL OVER ME, THANK YOU! SO LET'S FACE IT, HUSBAND, YOU HATE ME.
BUT I HAVE A QUESTION. MY LIFE. WHAT DECISION?
NO DECISION AS SUCH.
THE ARMY GAVE YOU TO ME. TO KILL. I AM THE WRONGED PARTY, AFTER ALL.
CAN I OFFER AN ARGUMENT? AGAINST MY OWN DEATH?
I DIDN'T COME FOR ARGUMENTS.

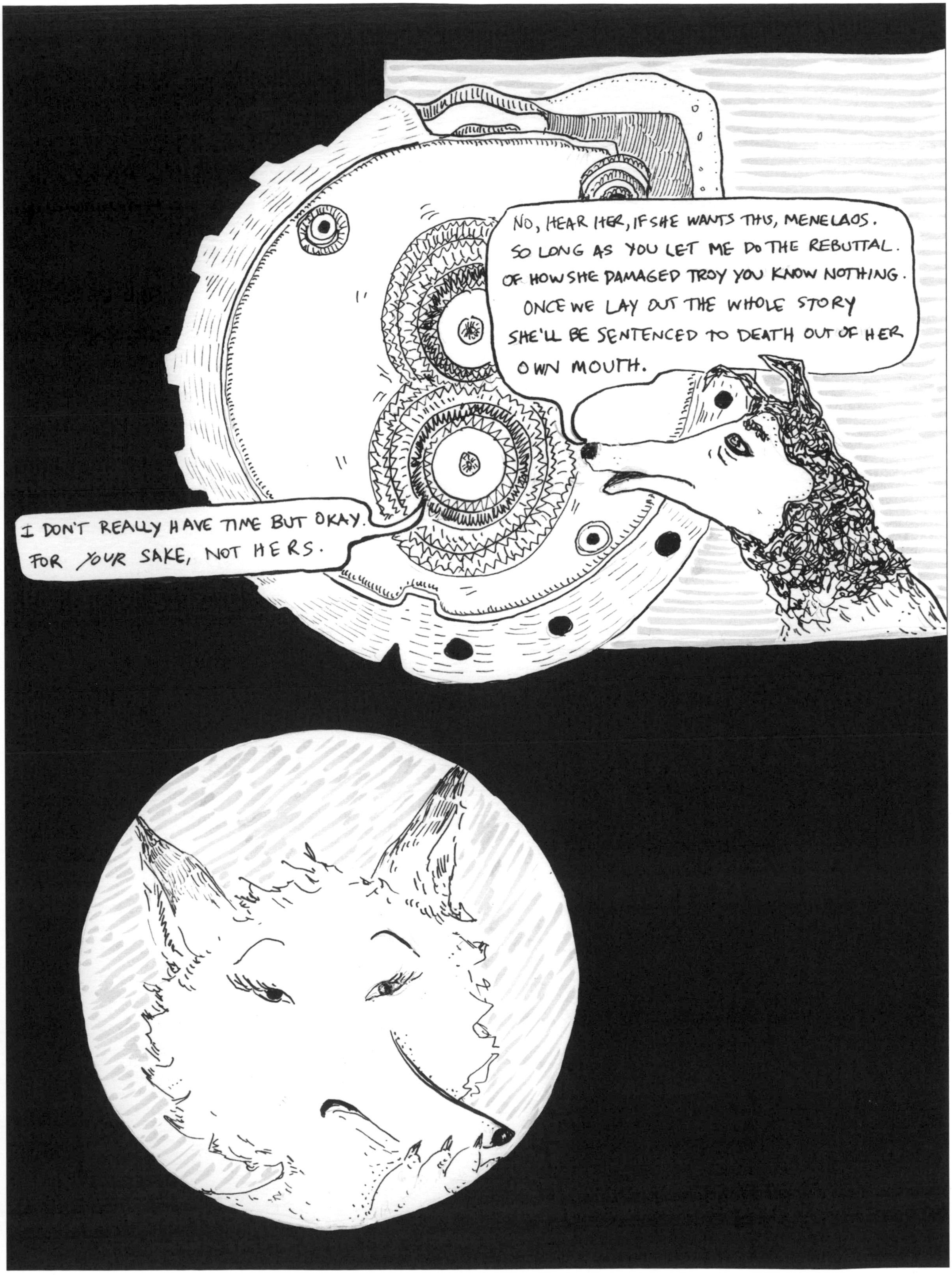

NO, HEAR HER, IF SHE WANTS THIS, MENELAOS. SO LONG AS YOU LET ME DO THE REBUTTAL. OF HOW SHE DAMAGED TROY YOU KNOW NOTHING. ONCE WE LAY OUT THE WHOLE STORY SHE'LL BE SENTENCED TO DEATH OUT OF HER OWN MOUTH.
I DON'T REALLY HAVE TIME BUT OKAY. FOR YOUR SAKE, NOT HERS.

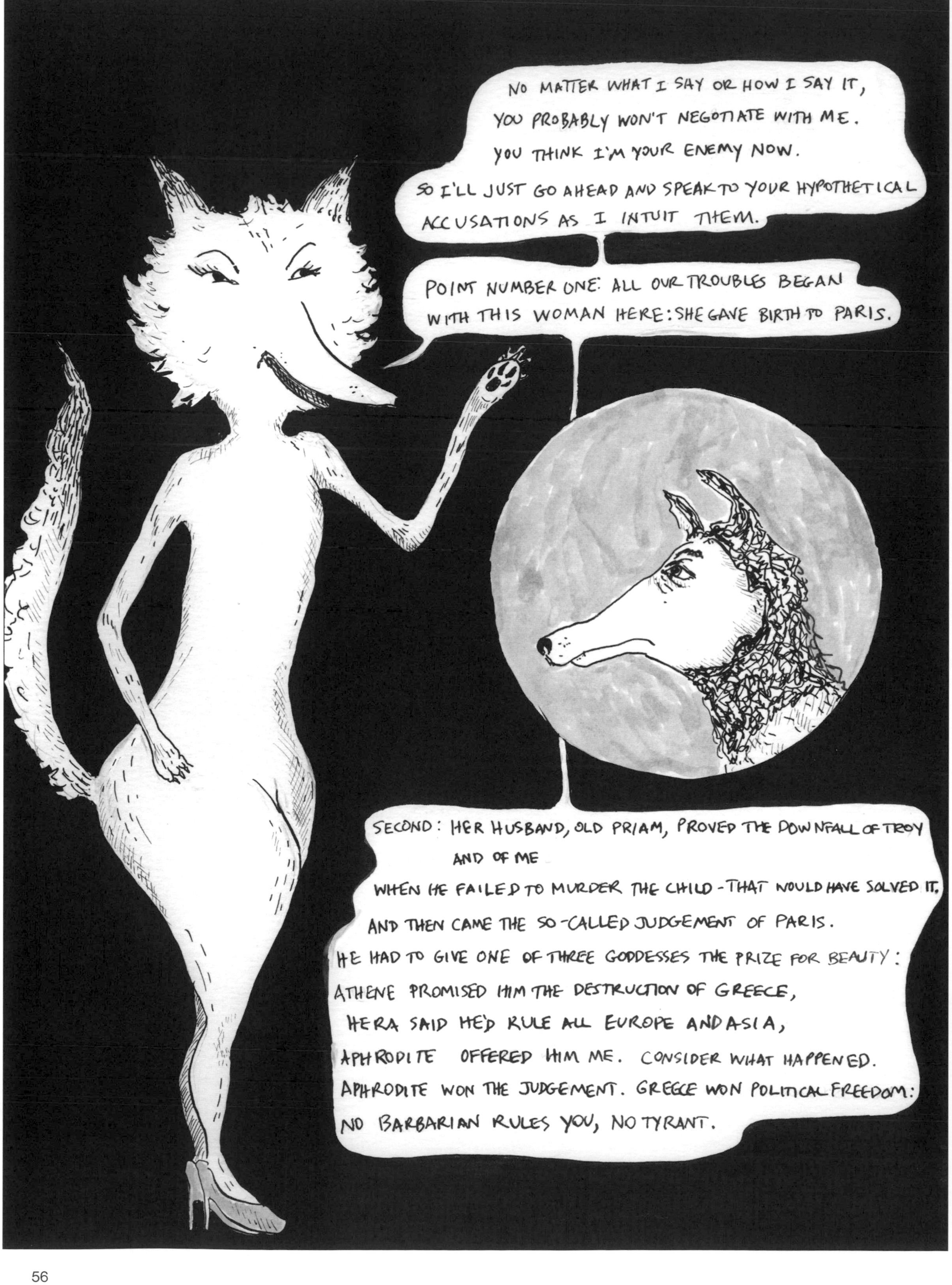
NO MATTER WHAT I SAY OR HOW I SAY IT, YOU PROBABLY WON'T NEGOTIATE WITH ME. YOU THINK I'M YOUR ENEMY NOW. SO I'LL JUST GO AHEAD AND SPEAK TO YOUR HYPOTHETICAL ACCUSATIONS AS I INTUIT THEM.
POINT NUMBER ONE: ALL OUR TROUBLES BEGAN WITH THIS WOMAN HERE: SHE GAVE BIRTH TO PARIS.
SECOND: HER HUSBAND, OLD PRIAM, PROVED THE DOWNFALL OF TROY AND OF ME WHEN HE FAILED TO MURDER THE CHILD - THAT WOULD HAVE SOLVED IT. AND THEN CAME THE SO-CALLED JUDGEMENT OF PARIS. HE HAD TO GIVE ONE OF THREE GODDESSES THE PRIZE FOR BEAUTY: ATHENE PROMISED HIM THE DESTRUCTION OF GREECE, HERA SAID HE'D RULE ALL EUROPE AND ASIA, APHRODITE OFFERED HIM ME. CONSIDER WHAT HAPPENED. APHRODITE WON THE JUDGEMENT. GREECE WON POLITICAL FREEDOM: NO BARBARIAN RULES YOU, NO TYRANT.

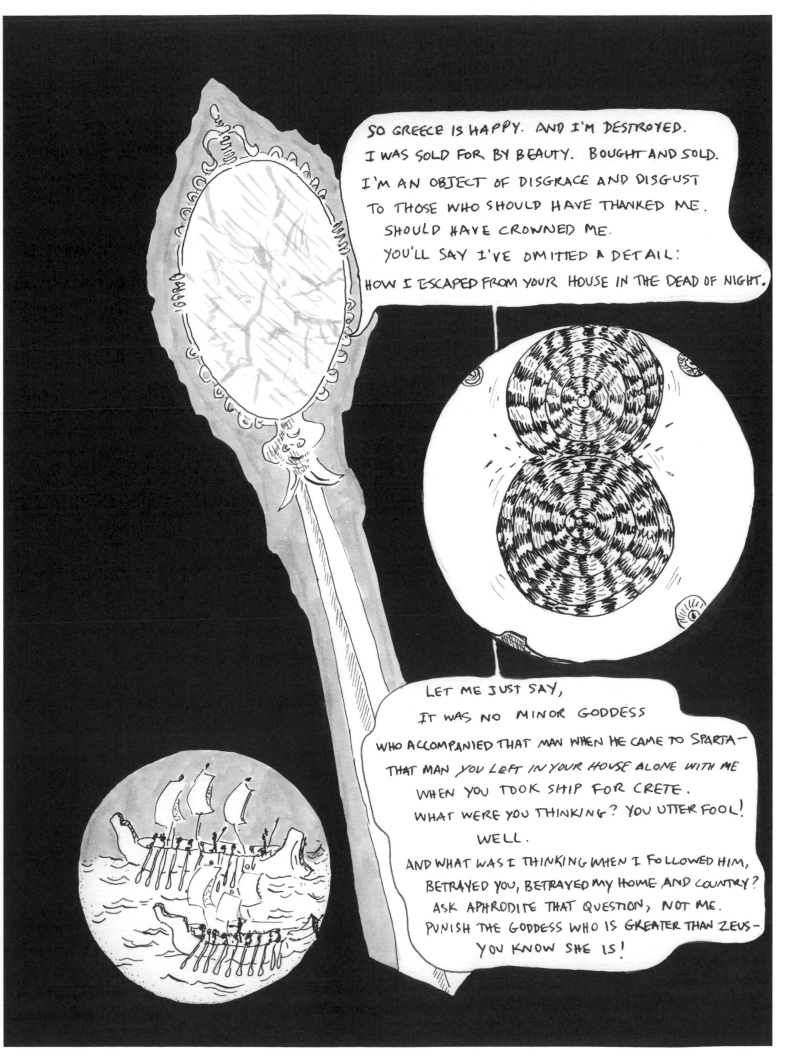

SO GREECE IS HAPPY. AND I'M DESTROYED.
I WAS SOLD FOR BY BEAUTY. BOUGHT AND SOLD.
I'M AN OBJECT OF DISGRACE AND DISGUST
TO THOSE WHO SHOULD HAVE THANKED ME.
SHOULD HAVE CROWNED ME.
YOU'LL SAY I'VE OMITTED A DETAIL:
HOW I ESCAPED FROM YOUR HOUSE IN THE DEAD OF NIGHT.

LET ME JUST SAY,
IT WAS NO MINOR GODDESS
WHO ACCOMPANIED THAT MAN WHEN HE CAME TO SPARTA—
THAT MAN YOU LEFT IN YOUR HOUSE ALONE WITH ME
WHEN YOU TOOK SHIP FOR CRETE.
WHAT WERE YOU THINKING? YOU UTTER FOOL!
WELL.
AND WHAT WAS I THINKING WHEN I FOLLOWED HIM,
BETRAYED YOU, BETRAYED MY HOME AND COUNTRY?
ASK APHRODITE THAT QUESTION, NOT ME.
PUNISH THE GODDESS WHO IS GREATER THAN ZEUS—
YOU KNOW SHE IS!

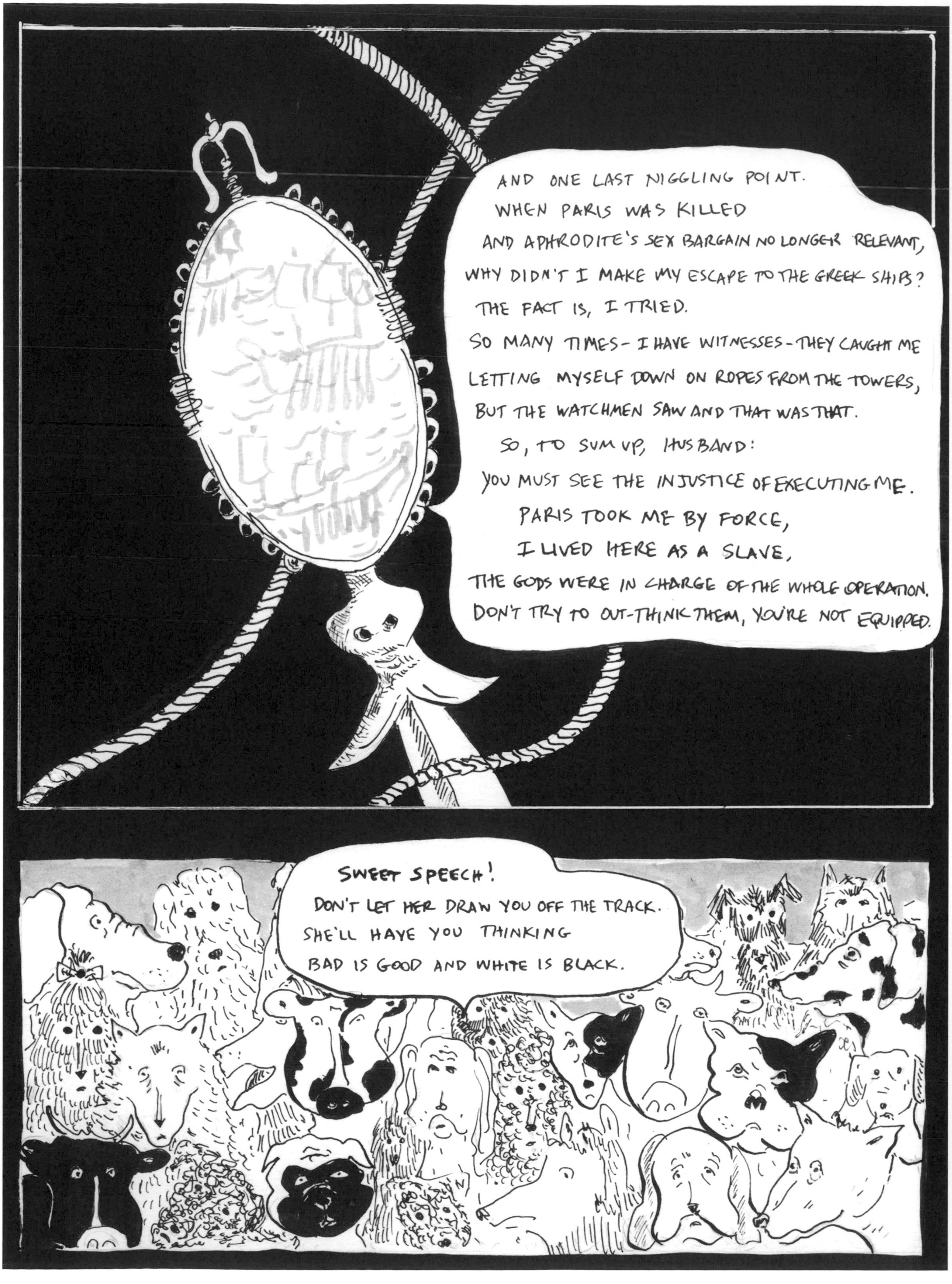
AND ONE LAST NIGGLING POINT.
WHEN PARIS WAS KILLED
AND APHRODITE'S SEX BARGAIN NO LONGER RELEVANT,
WHY DIDN'T I MAKE MY ESCAPE TO THE GREEK SHIPS?
THE FACT IS, I TRIED.
SO MANY TIMES - I HAVE WITNESSES - THEY CAUGHT ME
LETTING MYSELF DOWN ON ROPES FROM THE TOWERS,
BUT THE WATCHMEN SAW AND THAT WAS THAT.
SO, TO SUM UP, HUSBAND:
YOU MUST SEE THE INJUSTICE OF EXECUTING ME.
PARIS TOOK ME BY FORCE,
I LIVED HERE AS A SLAVE,
THE GODS WERE IN CHARGE OF THE WHOLE OPERATION.
DON'T TRY TO OUT-THINK THEM, YOU'RE NOT EQUIPPED.
SWEET SPEECH!
DON'T LET HER DRAW YOU OFF THE TRACK.
SHE'LL HAVE YOU THINKING
BAD IS GOOD AND WHITE IS BLACK.

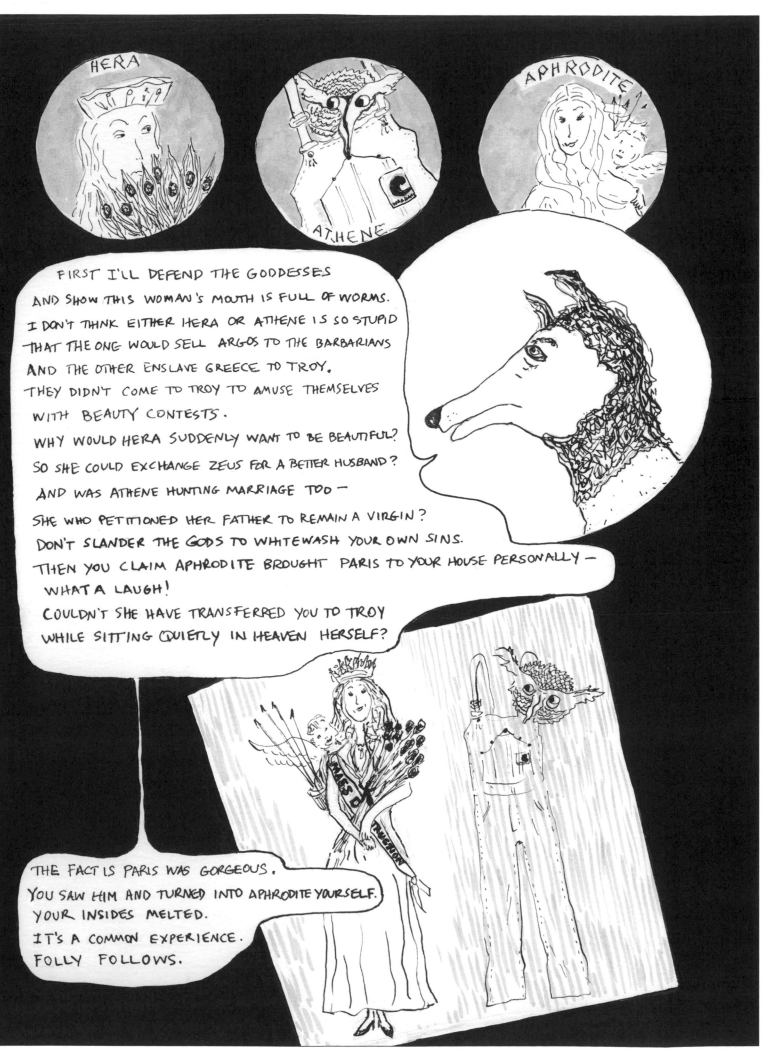

FIRST I'LL DEFEND THE GODDESSES
AND SHOW THIS WOMAN'S MOUTH IS FULL OF WORMS.
I DON'T THINK EITHER HERA OR ATHENE IS SO STUPID
THAT THE ONE WOULD SELL ARGOS TO THE BARBARIANS
AND THE OTHER ENSLAVE GREECE TO TROY.
THEY DIDN'T COME TO TROY TO AMUSE THEMSELVES
WITH BEAUTY CONTESTS.
WHY WOULD HERA SUDDENLY WANT TO BE BEAUTIFUL?
SO SHE COULD EXCHANGE ZEUS FOR A BETTER HUSBAND?
AND WAS ATHENE HUNTING MARRIAGE TOO —
SHE WHO PETITIONED HER FATHER TO REMAIN A VIRGIN?
DON'T SLANDER THE GODS TO WHITEWASH YOUR OWN SINS.
THEN YOU CLAIM APHRODITE BROUGHT PARIS TO YOUR HOUSE PERSONALLY —
WHAT A LAUGH!
COULDN'T SHE HAVE TRANSFERRED YOU TO TROY
WHILE SITTING QUIETLY IN HEAVEN HERSELF?

THE FACT IS PARIS WAS GORGEOUS.
YOU SAW HIM AND TURNED INTO APHRODITE YOURSELF.
YOUR INSIDES MELTED.
IT'S A COMMON EXPERIENCE.
FOLLY FOLLOWS.

HERA

ATHENE

APHRODITE

59

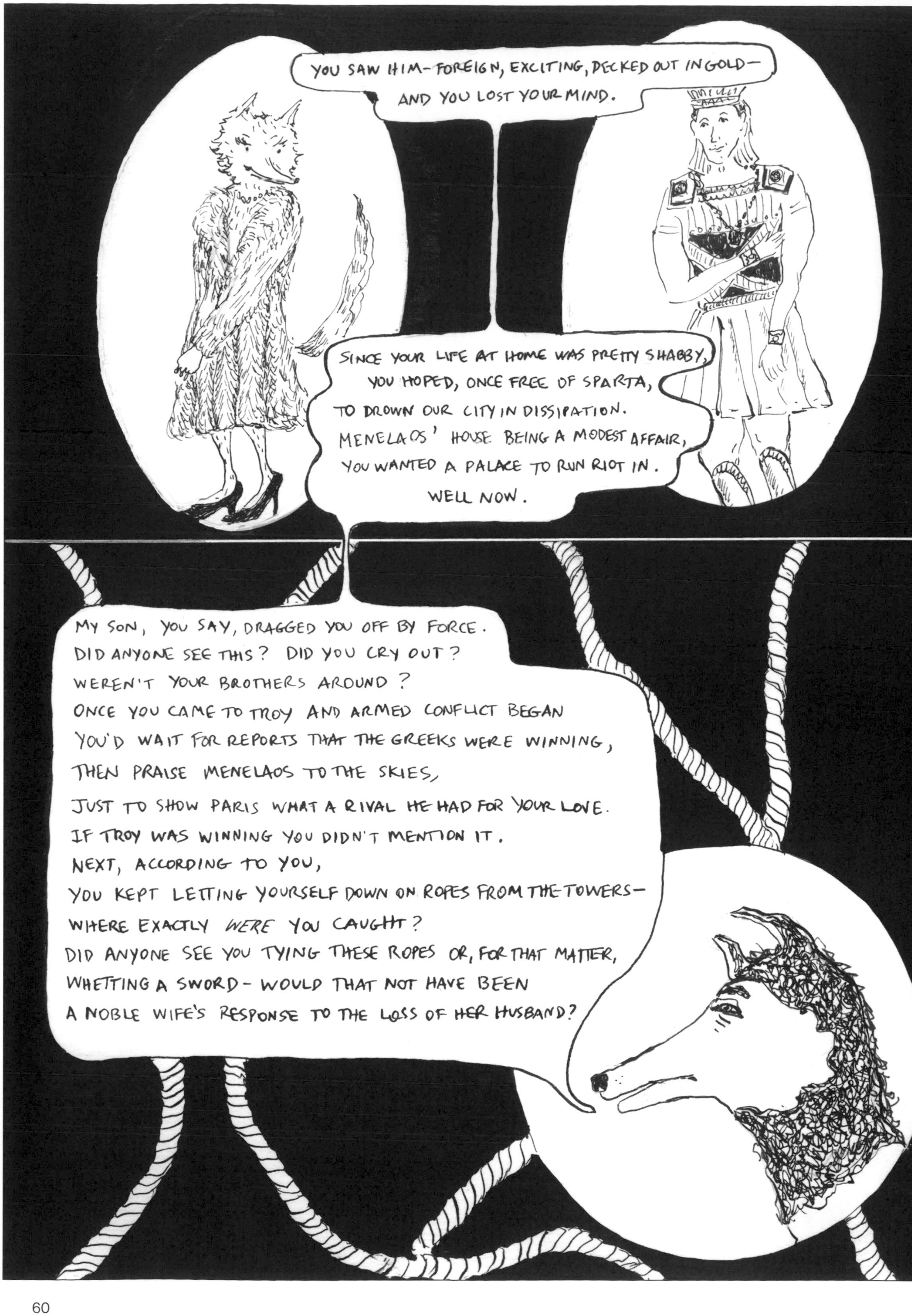
YOU SAW HIM—FOREIGN, EXCITING, DECKED OUT IN GOLD—AND YOU LOST YOUR MIND.
SINCE YOUR LIFE AT HOME WAS PRETTY SHABBY, YOU HOPED, ONCE FREE OF SPARTA, TO DROWN OUR CITY IN DISSIPATION. MENELAOS' HOUSE BEING A MODEST AFFAIR, YOU WANTED A PALACE TO RUN RIOT IN. WELL NOW.
MY SON, YOU SAY, DRAGGED YOU OFF BY FORCE. DID ANYONE SEE THIS? DID YOU CRY OUT? WEREN'T YOUR BROTHERS AROUND? ONCE YOU CAME TO TROY AND ARMED CONFLICT BEGAN YOU'D WAIT FOR REPORTS THAT THE GREEKS WERE WINNING, THEN PRAISE MENELAOS TO THE SKIES, JUST TO SHOW PARIS WHAT A RIVAL HE HAD FOR YOUR LOVE. IF TROY WAS WINNING YOU DIDN'T MENTION IT. NEXT, ACCORDING TO YOU, YOU KEPT LETTING YOURSELF DOWN ON ROPES FROM THE TOWERS—WHERE EXACTLY *WERE* YOU CAUGHT? DID ANYONE SEE YOU TYING THESE ROPES OR, FOR THAT MATTER, WHETTING A SWORD—WOULD THAT NOT HAVE BEEN A NOBLE WIFE'S RESPONSE TO THE LOSS OF HER HUSBAND?

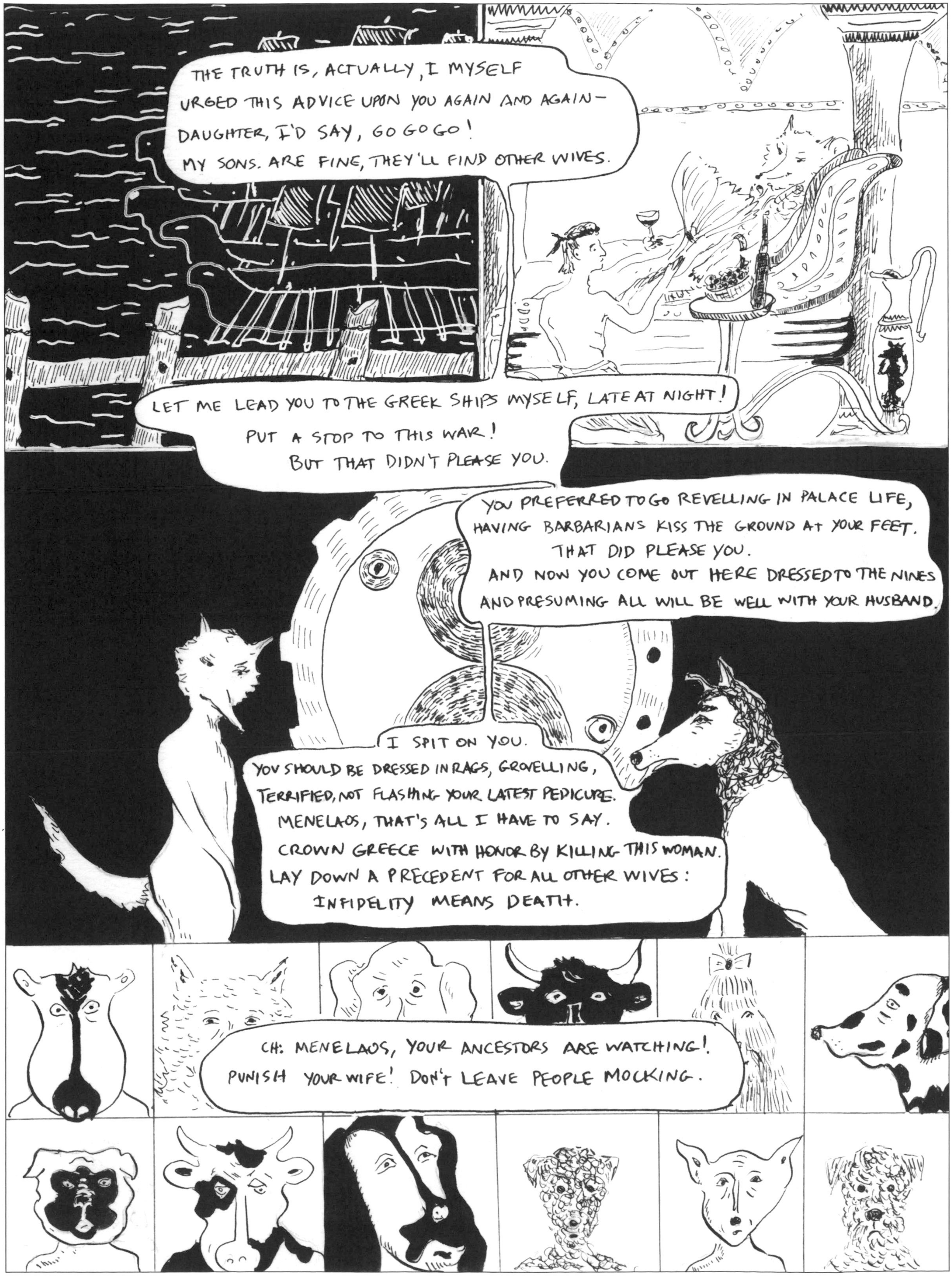
THE TRUTH IS, ACTUALLY, I MYSELF URGED THIS ADVICE UPON YOU AGAIN AND AGAIN— DAUGHTER, I'D SAY, GO GO GO! MY SONS ARE FINE, THEY'LL FIND OTHER WIVES.
LET ME LEAD YOU TO THE GREEK SHIPS MYSELF, LATE AT NIGHT! PUT A STOP TO THIS WAR! BUT THAT DIDN'T PLEASE YOU.
YOU PREFERRED TO GO REVELLING IN PALACE LIFE, HAVING BARBARIANS KISS THE GROUND AT YOUR FEET. THAT DID PLEASE YOU. AND NOW YOU COME OUT HERE DRESSED TO THE NINES AND PRESUMING ALL WILL BE WELL WITH YOUR HUSBAND.
I SPIT ON YOU. YOU SHOULD BE DRESSED IN RAGS, GROVELLING, TERRIFIED, NOT FLASHING YOUR LATEST PEDICURE. MENELAOS, THAT'S ALL I HAVE TO SAY. CROWN GREECE WITH HONOR BY KILLING THIS WOMAN. LAY DOWN A PRECEDENT FOR ALL OTHER WIVES: INFIDELITY MEANS DEATH.
CH: MENELAOS, YOUR ANCESTORS ARE WATCHING! PUNISH YOUR WIFE! DON'T LEAVE PEOPLE MOCKING.

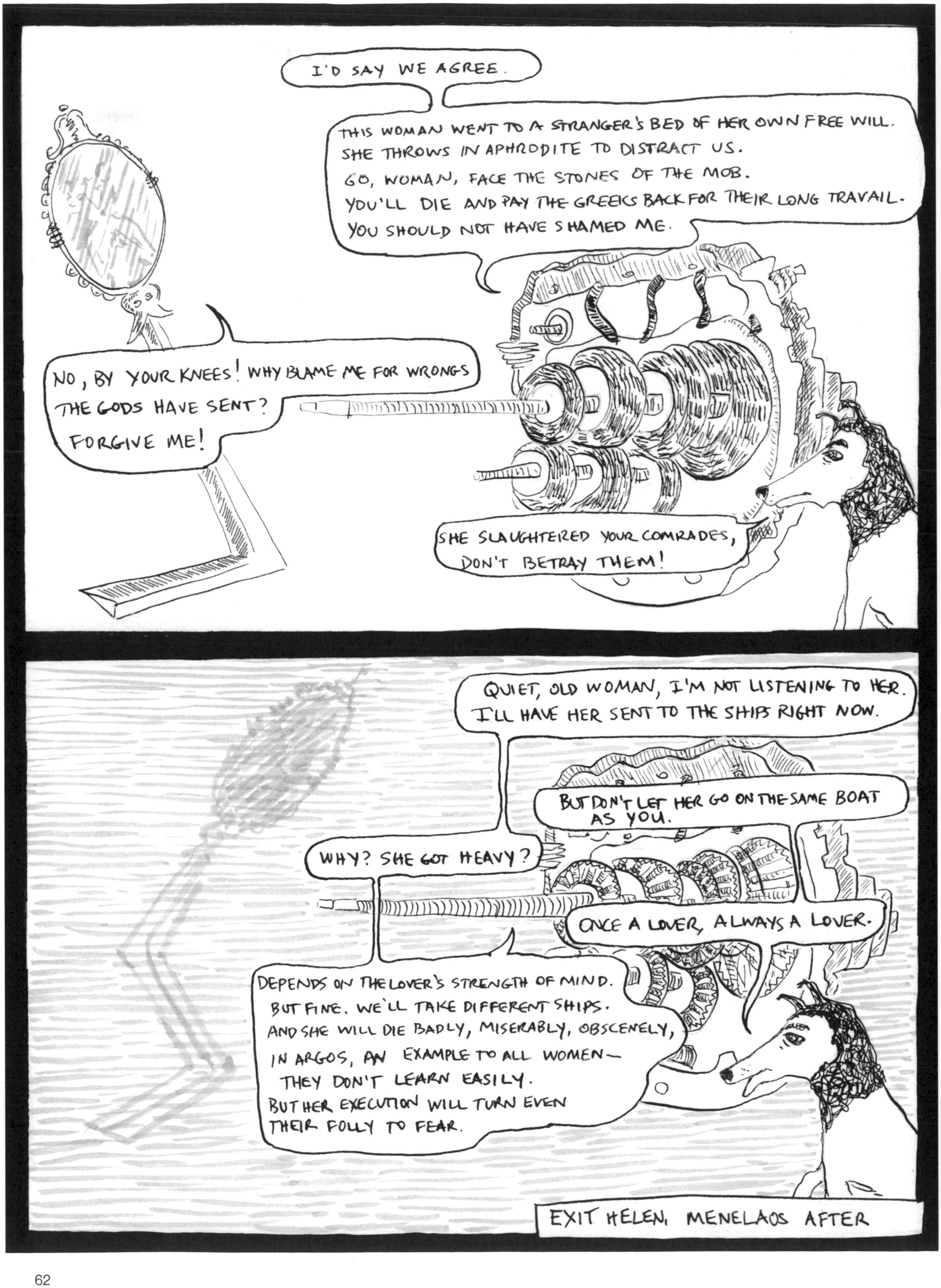
I'D SAY WE AGREE.
THIS WOMAN WENT TO A STRANGER'S BED OF HER OWN FREE WILL. SHE THROWS IN APHRODITE TO DISTRACT US. GO, WOMAN, FACE THE STONES OF THE MOB. YOU'LL DIE AND PAY THE GREEKS BACK FOR THEIR LONG TRAVAIL. YOU SHOULD NOT HAVE SHAMED ME.
NO, BY YOUR KNEES! WHY BLAME ME FOR WRONGS THE GODS HAVE SENT? FORGIVE ME!
SHE SLAUGHTERED YOUR COMRADES, DON'T BETRAY THEM!
QUIET, OLD WOMAN, I'M NOT LISTENING TO HER. I'LL HAVE HER SENT TO THE SHIPS RIGHT NOW.
BUT DON'T LET HER GO ON THE SAME BOAT AS YOU.
WHY? SHE GOT HEAVY?
ONCE A LOVER, ALWAYS A LOVER.
DEPENDS ON THE LOVER'S STRENGTH OF MIND. BUT FINE. WE'LL TAKE DIFFERENT SHIPS. AND SHE WILL DIE BADLY, MISERABLY, OBSCENELY, IN ARGOS, AN EXAMPLE TO ALL WOMEN— THEY DON'T LEARN EASILY. BUT HER EXECUTION WILL TURN EVEN THEIR FOLLY TO FEAR.
EXIT HELEN, MENELAOS AFTER

[redacted]

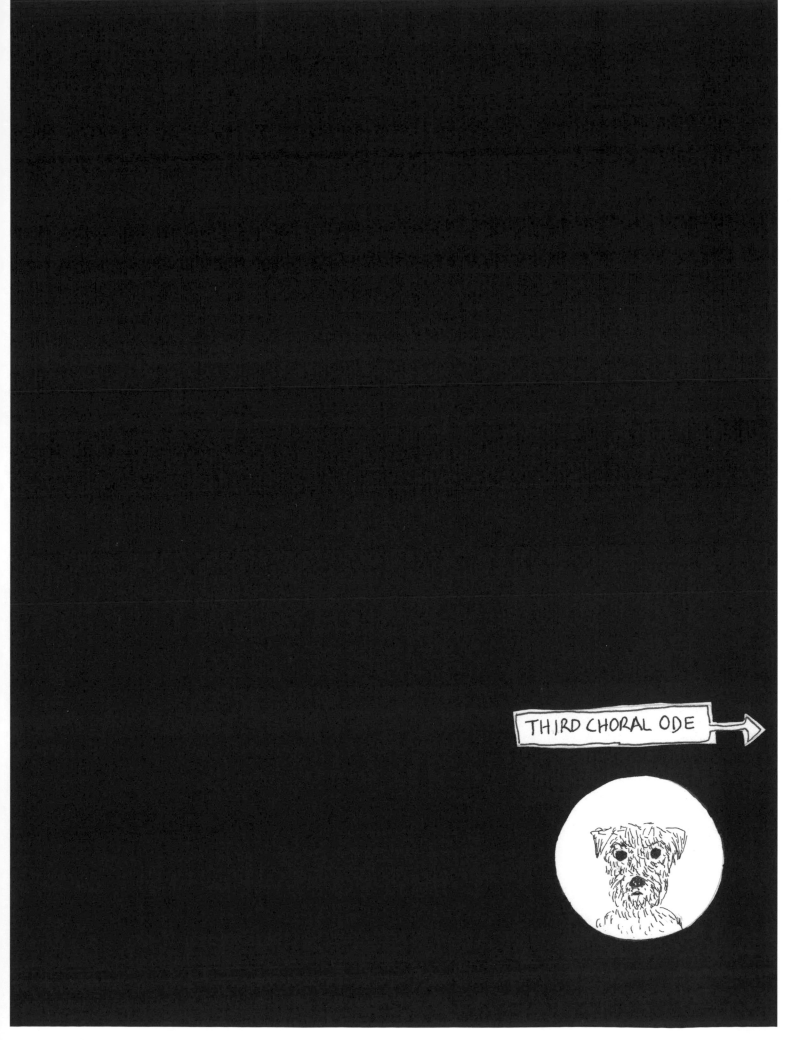

THIRD CHORAL ODE

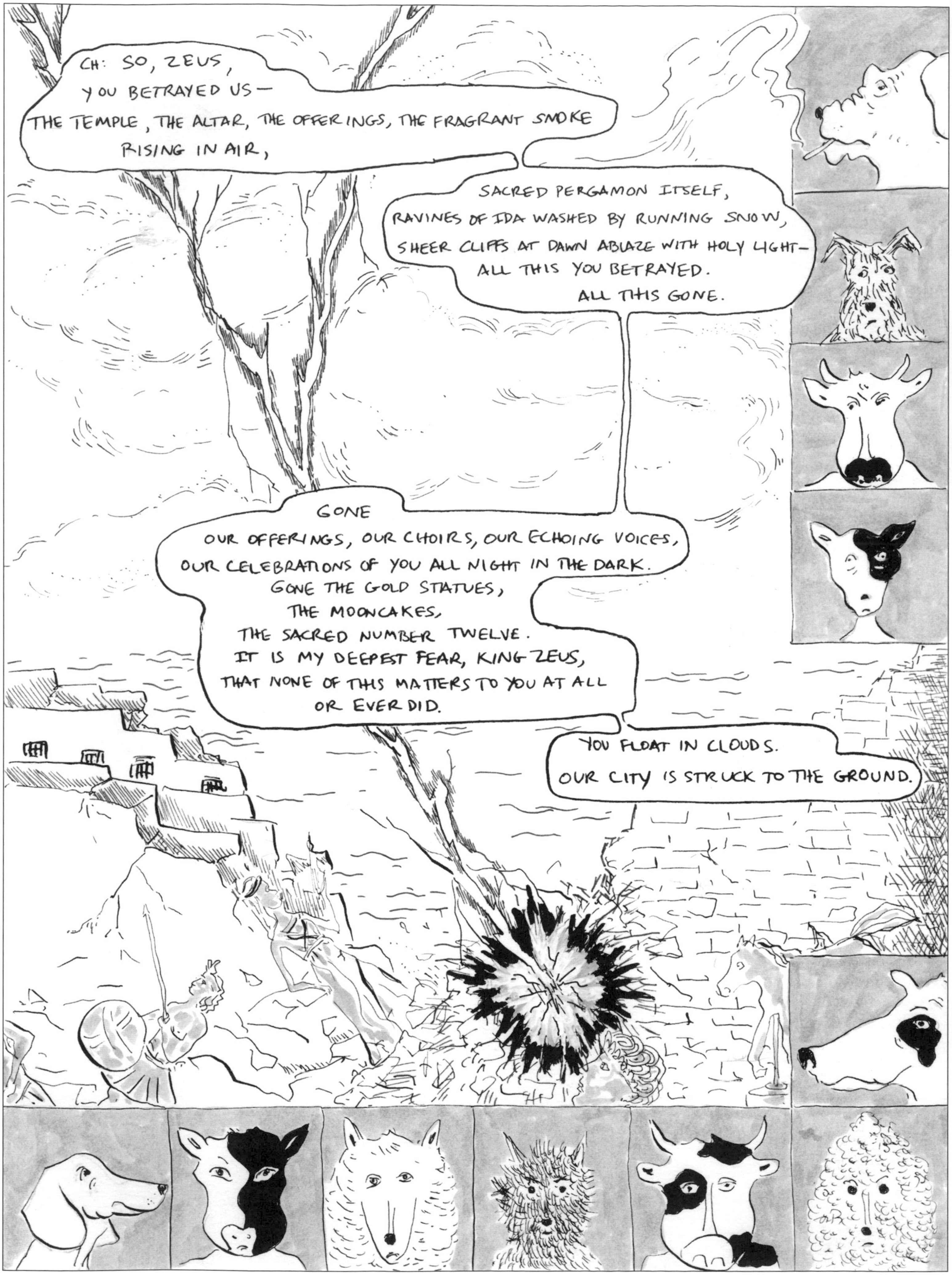
CH: SO, ZEUS,
YOU BETRAYED US—
THE TEMPLE, THE ALTAR, THE OFFERINGS, THE FRAGRANT SMOKE
RISING IN AIR,
SACRED PERGAMON ITSELF,
RAVINES OF IDA WASHED BY RUNNING SNOW,
SHEER CLIFFS AT DAWN ABLAZE WITH HOLY LIGHT—
ALL THIS YOU BETRAYED.
ALL THIS GONE.
GONE
OUR OFFERINGS, OUR CHOIRS, OUR ECHOING VOICES,
OUR CELEBRATIONS OF YOU ALL NIGHT IN THE DARK.
GONE THE GOLD STATUES,
THE MOONCAKES,
THE SACRED NUMBER TWELVE.
IT IS MY DEEPEST FEAR, KING ZEUS,
THAT NONE OF THIS MATTERS TO YOU AT ALL
OR EVER DID.
YOU FLOAT IN CLOUDS.
OUR CITY IS STRUCK TO THE GROUND.

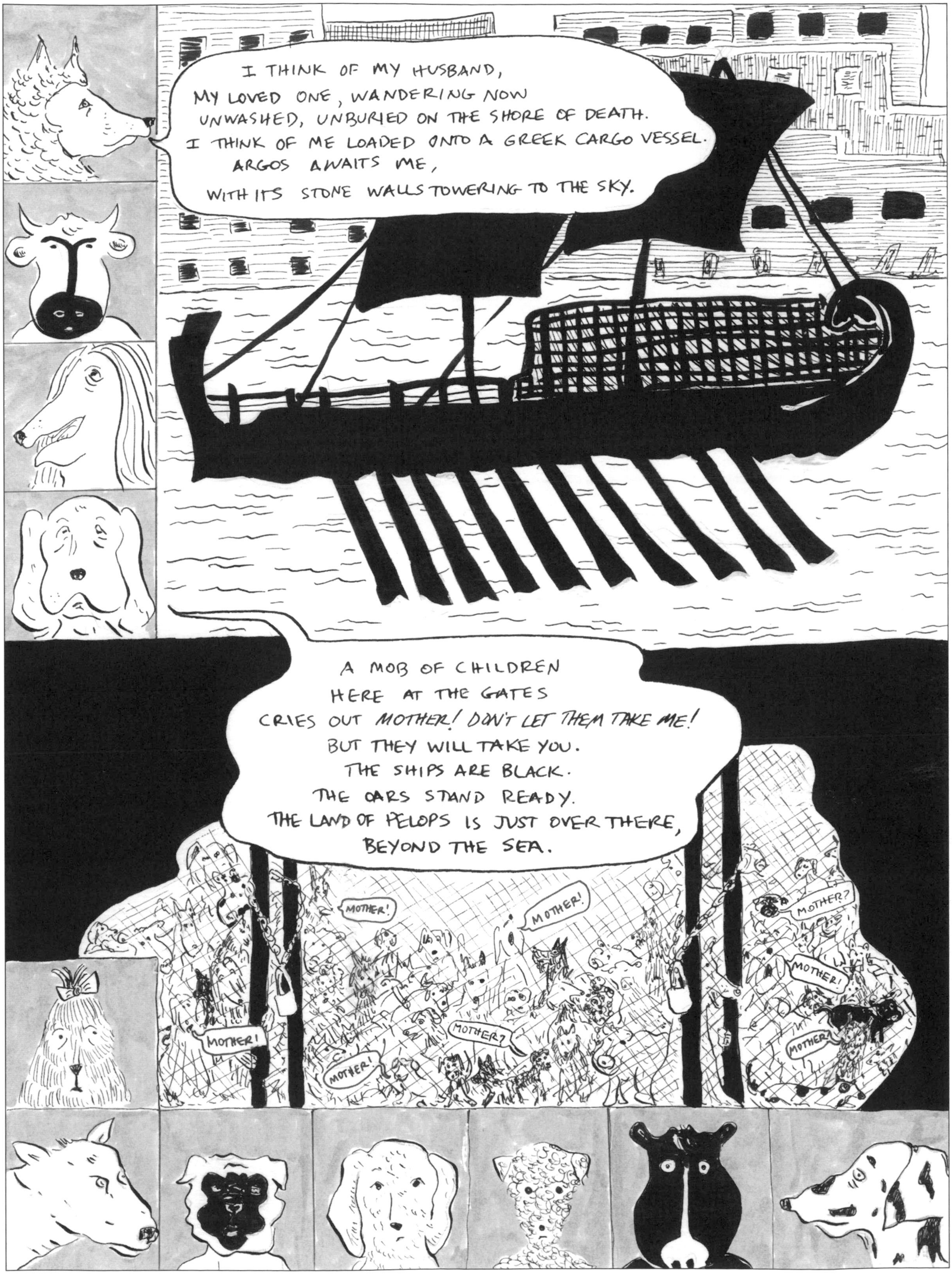
I THINK OF MY HUSBAND, MY LOVED ONE, WANDERING NOW UNWASHED, UNBURIED ON THE SHORE OF DEATH. I THINK OF ME LOADED ONTO A GREEK CARGO VESSEL. ARGOS AWAITS ME, WITH ITS STONE WALLS TOWERING TO THE SKY.
A MOB OF CHILDREN HERE AT THE GATES CRIES OUT *MOTHER! DON'T LET THEM TAKE ME!* BUT THEY WILL TAKE YOU. THE SHIPS ARE BLACK. THE OARS STAND READY. THE LAND OF PELOPS IS JUST OVER THERE, BEYOND THE SEA.
MOTHER!
MOTHER!
MOTHER?
MOTHER!
MOTHER!
MOTHER?
MOTHER!
MOTHER?

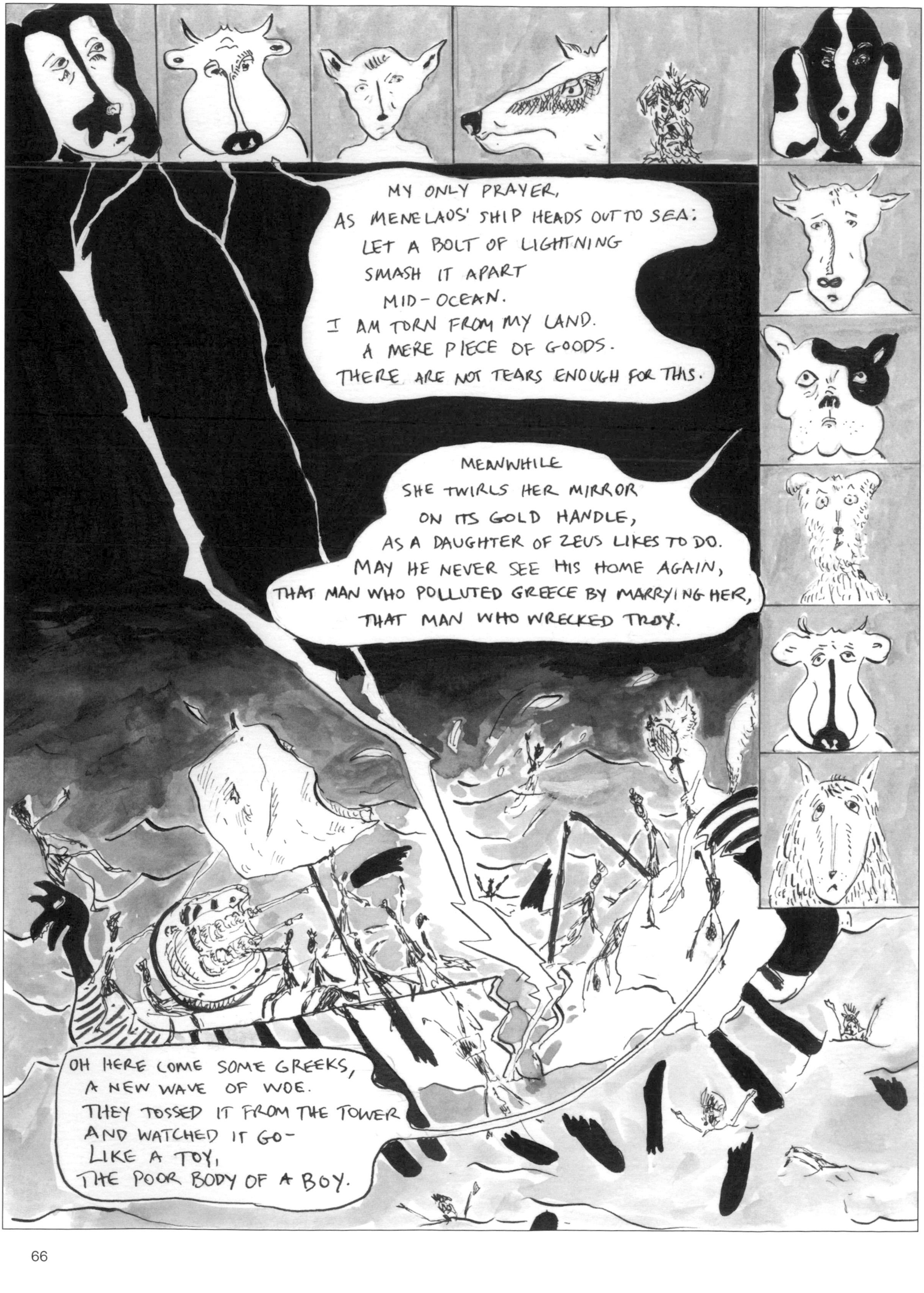
MY ONLY PRAYER, AS MENELAOS' SHIP HEADS OUT TO SEA: LET A BOLT OF LIGHTNING SMASH IT APART MID-OCEAN. I AM TORN FROM MY LAND. A MERE PIECE OF GOODS. THERE ARE NOT TEARS ENOUGH FOR THIS.
MEANWHILE SHE TWIRLS HER MIRROR ON ITS GOLD HANDLE, AS A DAUGHTER OF ZEUS LIKES TO DO. MAY HE NEVER SEE HIS HOME AGAIN, THAT MAN WHO POLLUTED GREECE BY MARRYING HER, THAT MAN WHO WRECKED TROY.
OH HERE COME SOME GREEKS, A NEW WAVE OF WOE. THEY TOSSED IT FROM THE TOWER AND WATCHED IT GO- LIKE A TOY, THE POOR BODY OF A BOY.

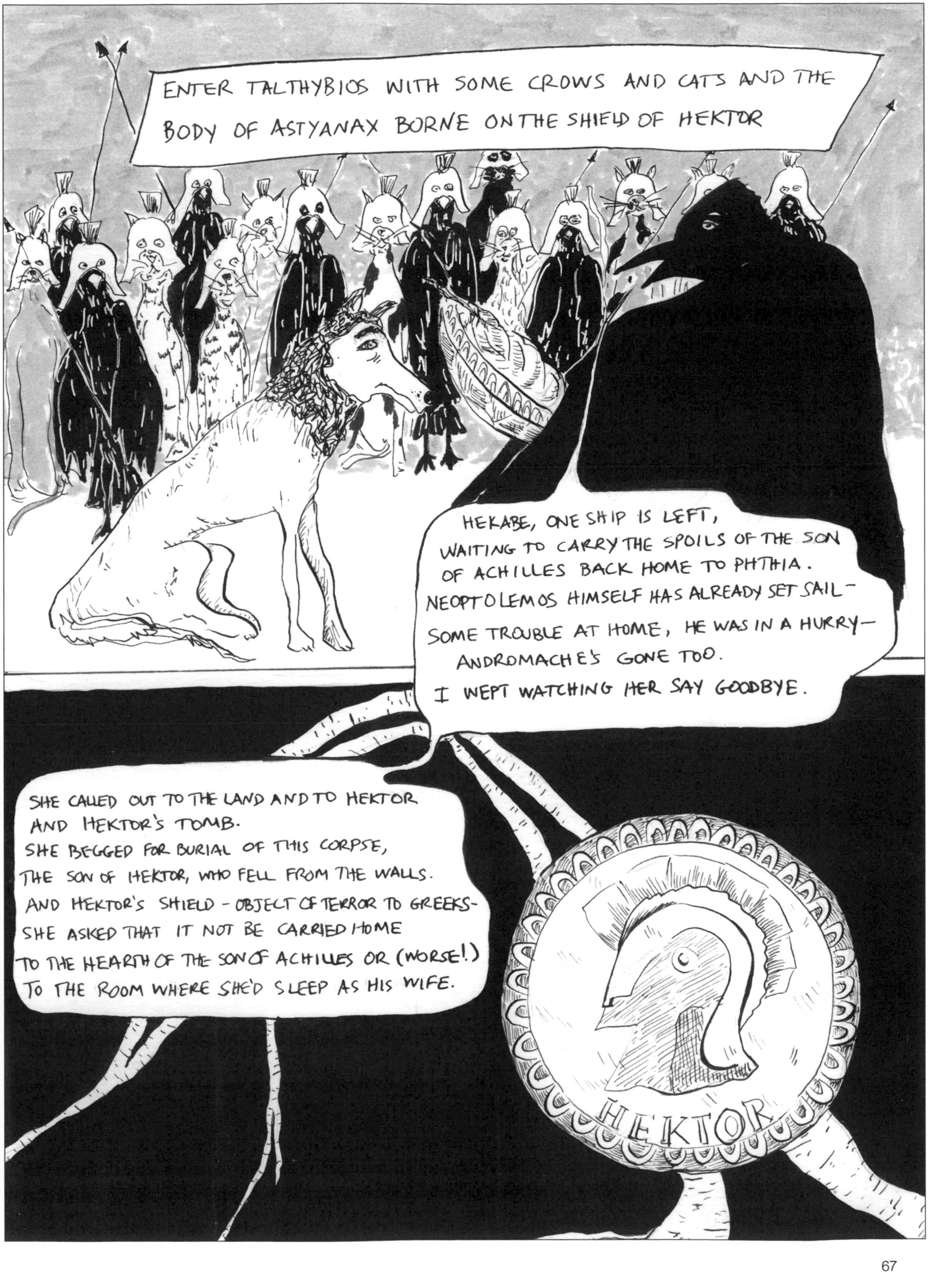
ENTER TALTHYBIOS WITH SOME CROWS AND CATS AND THE BODY OF ASTYANAX BORNE ON THE SHIELD OF HEKTOR
HEKABE, ONE SHIP IS LEFT, WAITING TO CARRY THE SPOILS OF THE SON OF ACHILLES BACK HOME TO PHTHIA. NEOPTOLEMOS HIMSELF HAS ALREADY SET SAIL— SOME TROUBLE AT HOME, HE WAS IN A HURRY— ANDROMACHE'S GONE TOO. I WEPT WATCHING HER SAY GOODBYE.
SHE CALLED OUT TO THE LAND AND TO HEKTOR AND HEKTOR'S TOMB. SHE BEGGED FOR BURIAL OF THIS CORPSE, THE SON OF HEKTOR, WHO FELL FROM THE WALLS. AND HEKTOR'S SHIELD - OBJECT OF TERROR TO GREEKS- SHE ASKED THAT IT NOT BE CARRIED HOME TO THE HEARTH OF THE SON OF ACHILLES OR (WORSE!) TO THE ROOM WHERE SHE'D SLEEP AS HIS WIFE.
HEKTOR

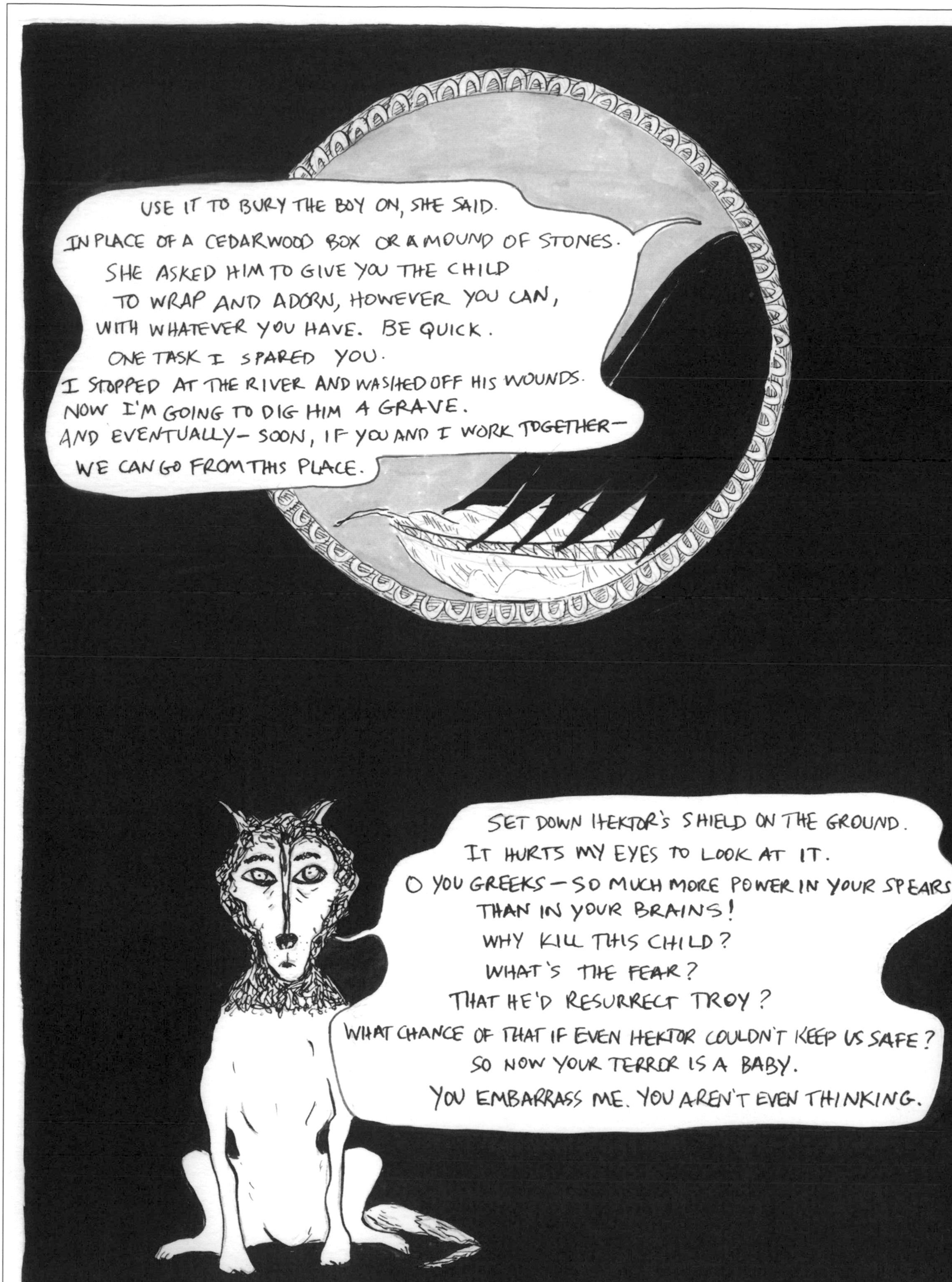
USE IT TO BURY THE BOY ON, SHE SAID. IN PLACE OF A CEDARWOOD BOX OR A MOUND OF STONES. SHE ASKED HIM TO GIVE YOU THE CHILD TO WRAP AND ADORN, HOWEVER YOU CAN, WITH WHATEVER YOU HAVE. BE QUICK. ONE TASK I SPARED YOU. I STOPPED AT THE RIVER AND WASHED OFF HIS WOUNDS. NOW I'M GOING TO DIG HIM A GRAVE. AND EVENTUALLY– SOON, IF YOU AND I WORK TOGETHER– WE CAN GO FROM THIS PLACE.
SET DOWN HEKTOR'S SHIELD ON THE GROUND. IT HURTS MY EYES TO LOOK AT IT. O YOU GREEKS – SO MUCH MORE POWER IN YOUR SPEARS THAN IN YOUR BRAINS! WHY KILL THIS CHILD? WHAT'S THE FEAR? THAT HE'D RESURRECT TROY? WHAT CHANCE OF THAT IF EVEN HEKTOR COULDN'T KEEP US SAFE? SO NOW YOUR TERROR IS A BABY. YOU EMBARRASS ME. YOU AREN'T EVEN THINKING.

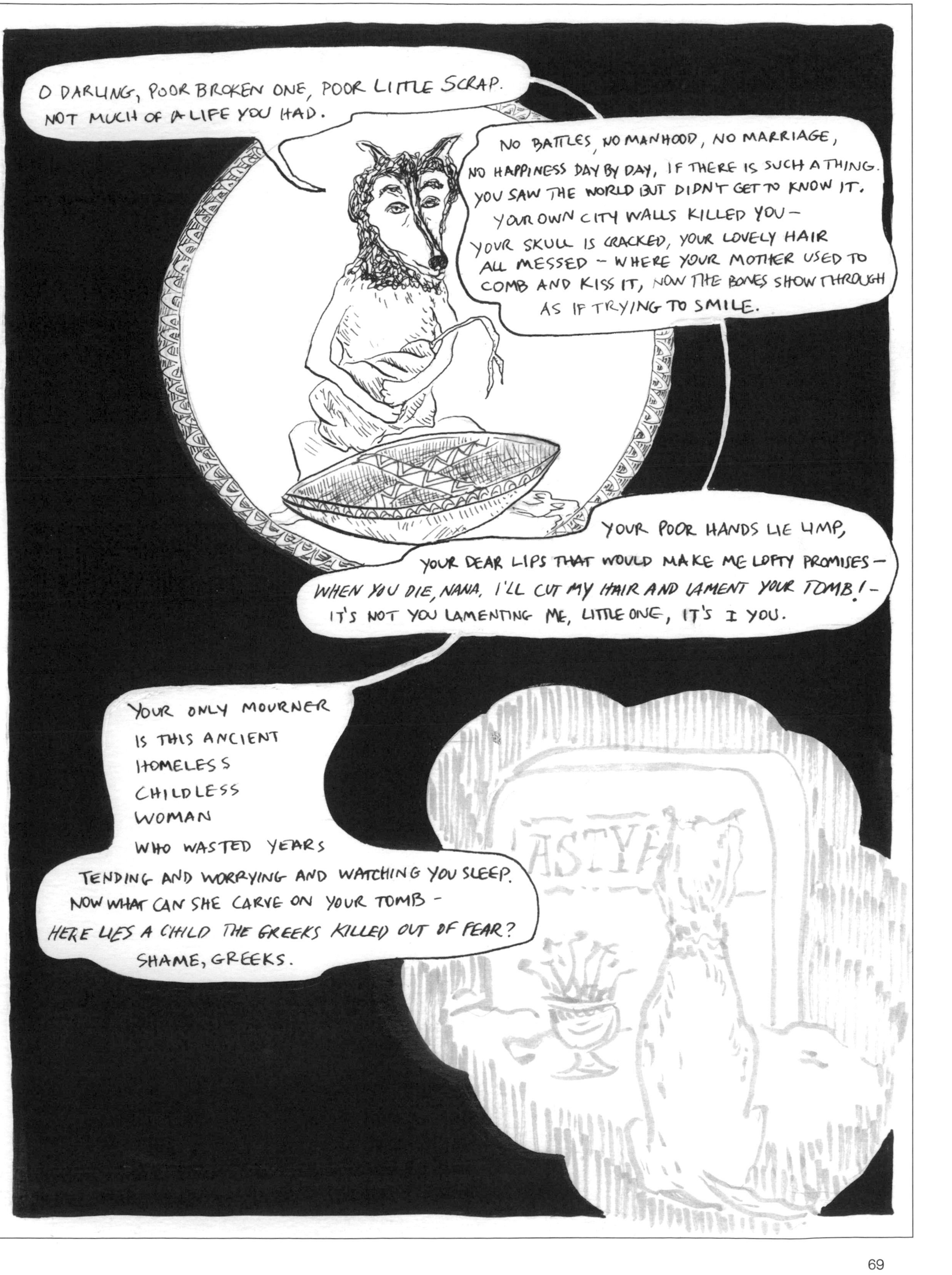
O DARLING, POOR BROKEN ONE, POOR LITTLE SCRAP. NOT MUCH OF A LIFE YOU HAD.
NO BATTLES, NO MANHOOD, NO MARRIAGE, NO HAPPINESS DAY BY DAY, IF THERE IS SUCH A THING. YOU SAW THE WORLD BUT DIDN'T GET TO KNOW IT. YOUR OWN CITY WALLS KILLED YOU — YOUR SKULL IS CRACKED, YOUR LOVELY HAIR ALL MESSED — WHERE YOUR MOTHER USED TO COMB AND KISS IT, NOW THE BONES SHOW THROUGH AS IF TRYING TO SMILE.
YOUR POOR HANDS LIE LIMP, YOUR DEAR LIPS THAT WOULD MAKE ME LOFTY PROMISES — WHEN YOU DIE, NANA, I'LL CUT MY HAIR AND LAMENT YOUR TOMB! — IT'S NOT YOU LAMENTING ME, LITTLE ONE, IT'S I YOU.
YOUR ONLY MOURNER IS THIS ANCIENT HOMELESS CHILDLESS WOMAN WHO WASTED YEARS TENDING AND WORRYING AND WATCHING YOU SLEEP. NOW WHAT CAN SHE CARVE ON YOUR TOMB — HERE LIES A CHILD THE GREEKS KILLED OUT OF FEAR? SHAME, GREEKS.
ASTYA

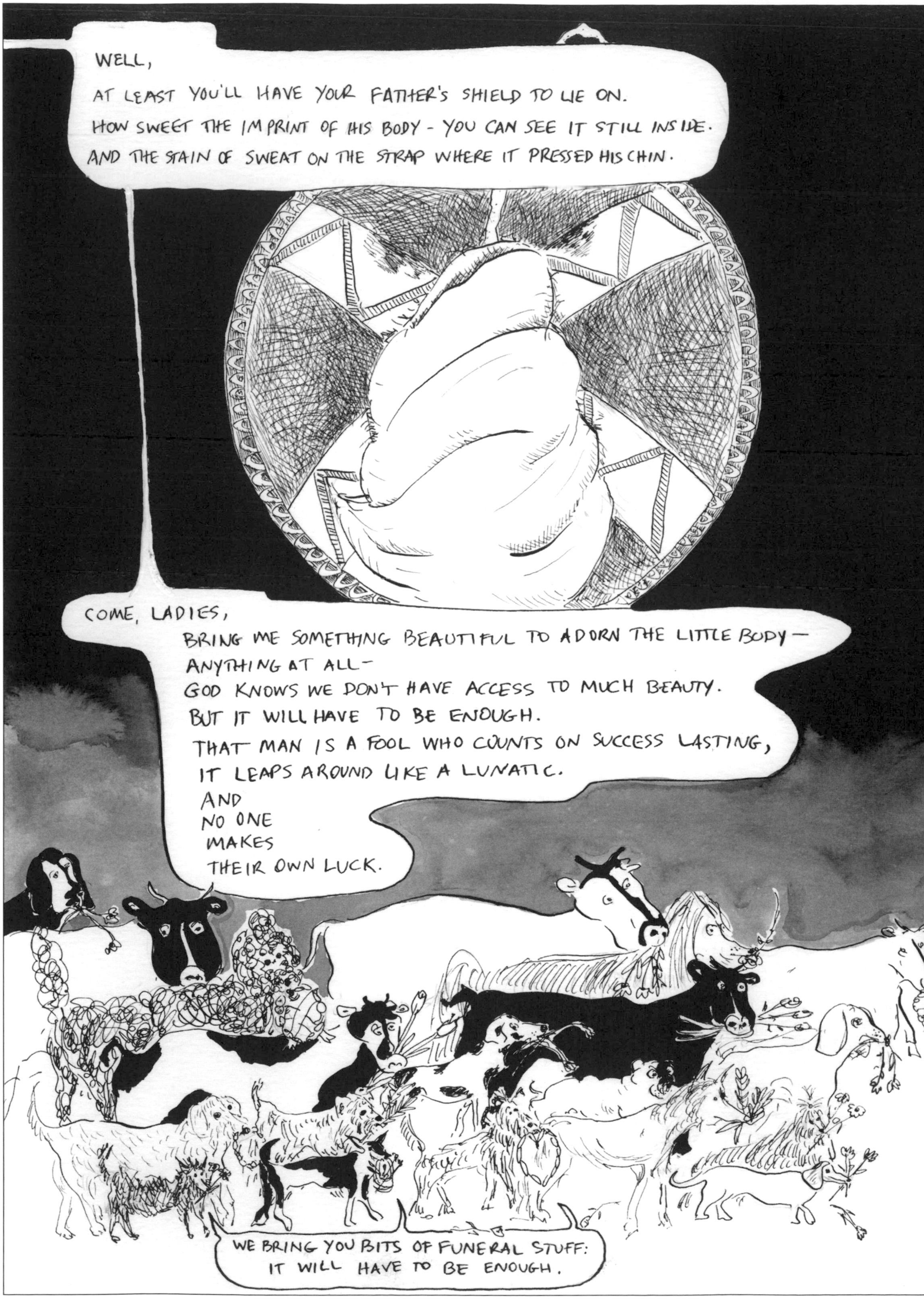
WELL,
AT LEAST YOU'LL HAVE YOUR FATHER'S SHIELD TO LIE ON.
HOW SWEET THE IMPRINT OF HIS BODY - YOU CAN SEE IT STILL INSIDE.
AND THE STAIN OF SWEAT ON THE STRAP WHERE IT PRESSED HIS CHIN.
COME, LADIES,
BRING ME SOMETHING BEAUTIFUL TO ADORN THE LITTLE BODY—
ANYTHING AT ALL—
GOD KNOWS WE DON'T HAVE ACCESS TO MUCH BEAUTY.
BUT IT WILL HAVE TO BE ENOUGH.
THAT MAN IS A FOOL WHO COUNTS ON SUCCESS LASTING,
IT LEAPS AROUND LIKE A LUNATIC.
AND
NO ONE
MAKES
THEIR OWN LUCK.
WE BRING YOU BITS OF FUNERAL STUFF:
IT WILL HAVE TO BE ENOUGH.

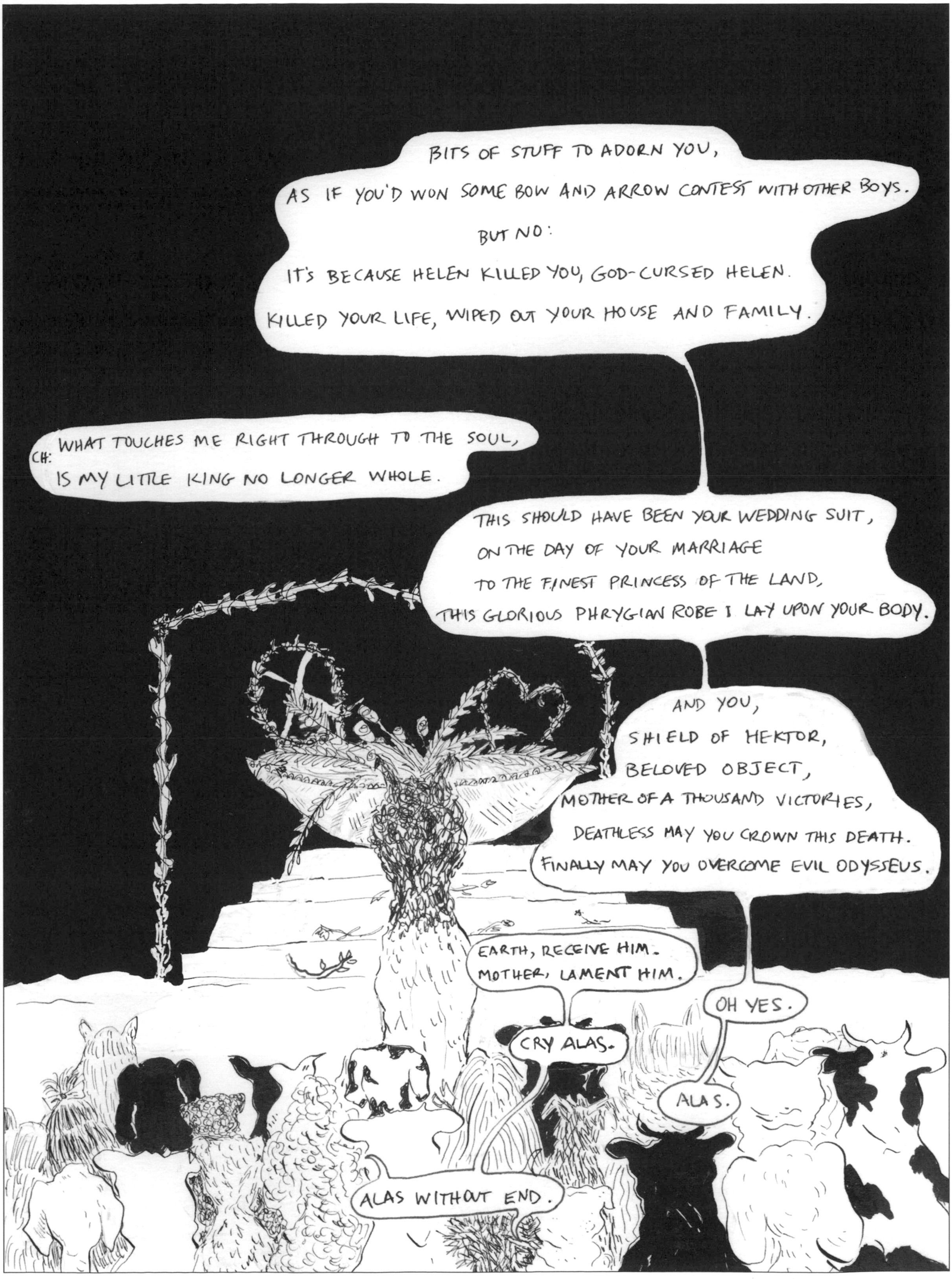
BITS OF STUFF TO ADORN YOU,
AS IF YOU'D WON SOME BOW AND ARROW CONTEST WITH OTHER BOYS.
BUT NO:
IT'S BECAUSE HELEN KILLED YOU, GOD-CURSED HELEN.
KILLED YOUR LIFE, WIPED OUT YOUR HOUSE AND FAMILY.
CH: WHAT TOUCHES ME RIGHT THROUGH TO THE SOUL,
IS MY LITTLE KING NO LONGER WHOLE.
THIS SHOULD HAVE BEEN YOUR WEDDING SUIT,
ON THE DAY OF YOUR MARRIAGE
TO THE FINEST PRINCESS OF THE LAND,
THIS GLORIOUS PHRYGIAN ROBE I LAY UPON YOUR BODY.
AND YOU,
SHIELD OF HEKTOR,
BELOVED OBJECT,
MOTHER OF A THOUSAND VICTORIES,
DEATHLESS MAY YOU CROWN THIS DEATH.
FINALLY MAY YOU OVERCOME EVIL ODYSSEUS.
EARTH, RECEIVE HIM.
MOTHER, LAMENT HIM.
OH YES.
CRY ALAS.
ALAS.
ALAS WITHOUT END.

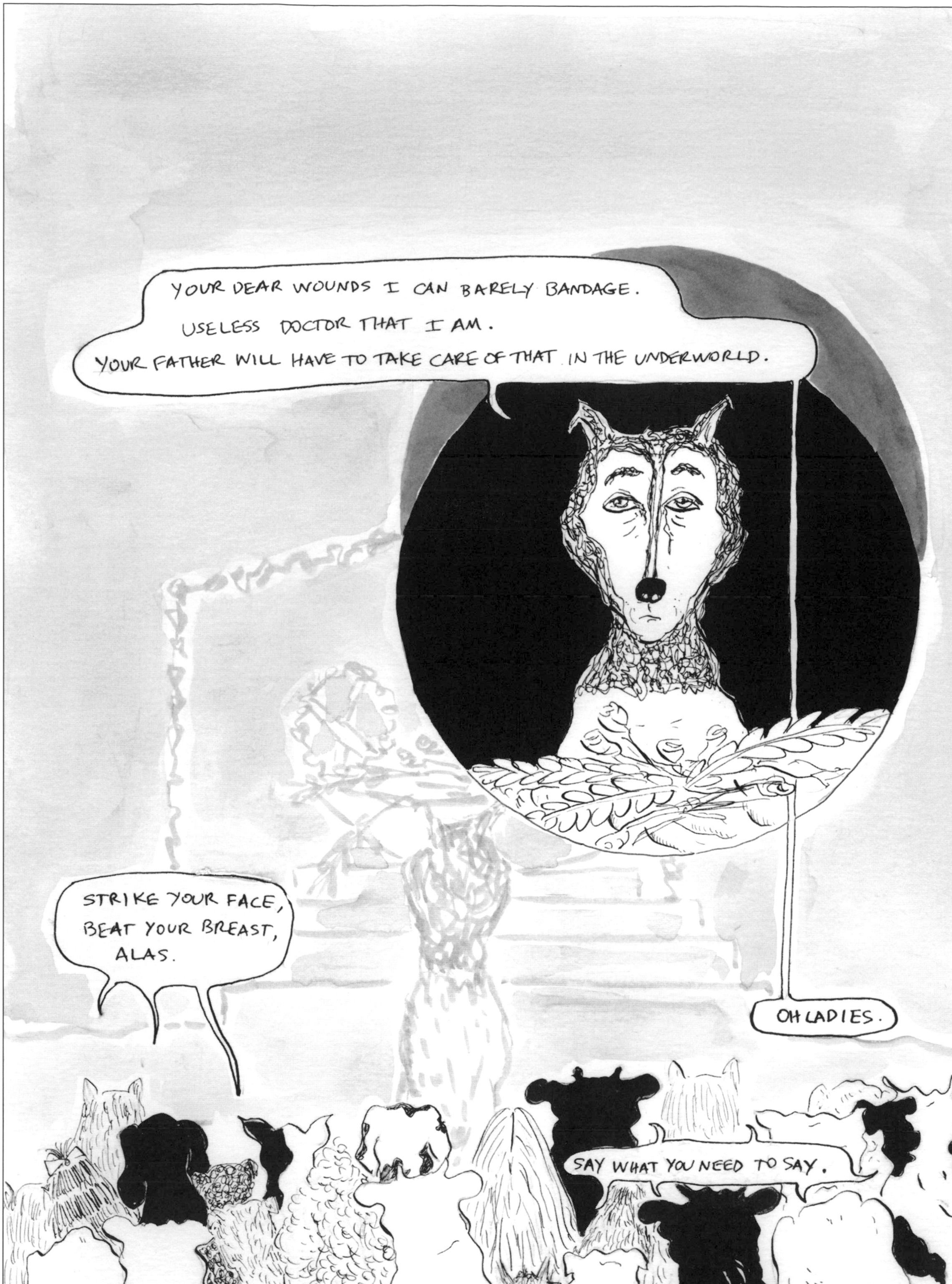
YOUR DEAR WOUNDS I CAN BARELY BANDAGE.
USELESS DOCTOR THAT I AM.
YOUR FATHER WILL HAVE TO TAKE CARE OF THAT IN THE UNDERWORLD.
STRIKE YOUR FACE, BEAT YOUR BREAST, ALAS.
OH LADIES.
SAY WHAT YOU NEED TO SAY.

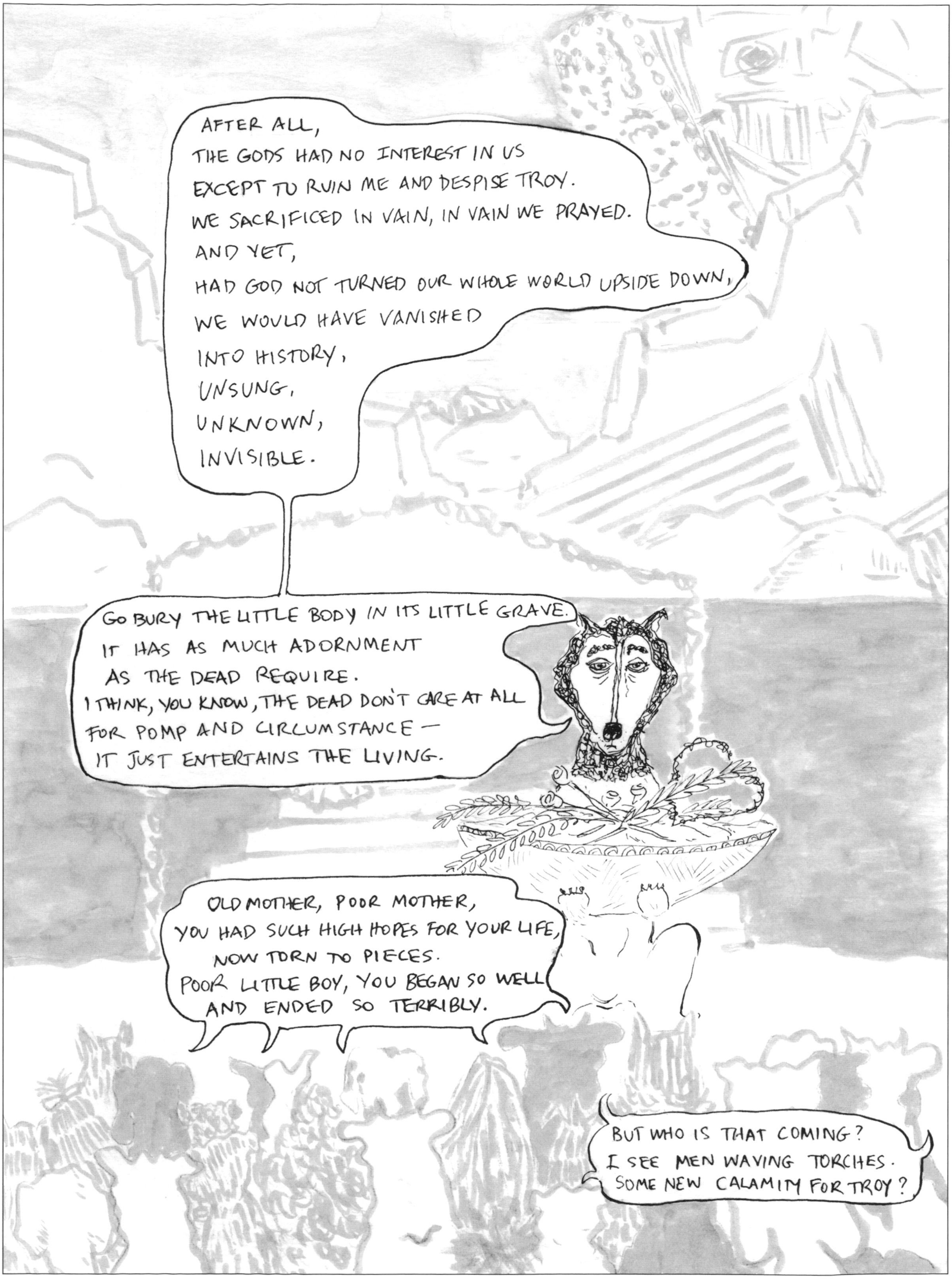
AFTER ALL, THE GODS HAD NO INTEREST IN US EXCEPT TO RUIN ME AND DESPISE TROY. WE SACRIFICED IN VAIN, IN VAIN WE PRAYED. AND YET, HAD GOD NOT TURNED OUR WHOLE WORLD UPSIDE DOWN, WE WOULD HAVE VANISHED INTO HISTORY, UNSUNG, UNKNOWN, INVISIBLE.
GO BURY THE LITTLE BODY IN ITS LITTLE GRAVE. IT HAS AS MUCH ADORNMENT AS THE DEAD REQUIRE. I THINK, YOU KNOW, THE DEAD DON'T CARE AT ALL FOR POMP AND CIRCUMSTANCE — IT JUST ENTERTAINS THE LIVING.
OLD MOTHER, POOR MOTHER, YOU HAD SUCH HIGH HOPES FOR YOUR LIFE, NOW TORN TO PIECES. POOR LITTLE BOY, YOU BEGAN SO WELL AND ENDED SO TERRIBLY.
BUT WHO IS THAT COMING? I SEE MEN WAVING TORCHES. SOME NEW CALAMITY FOR TROY?

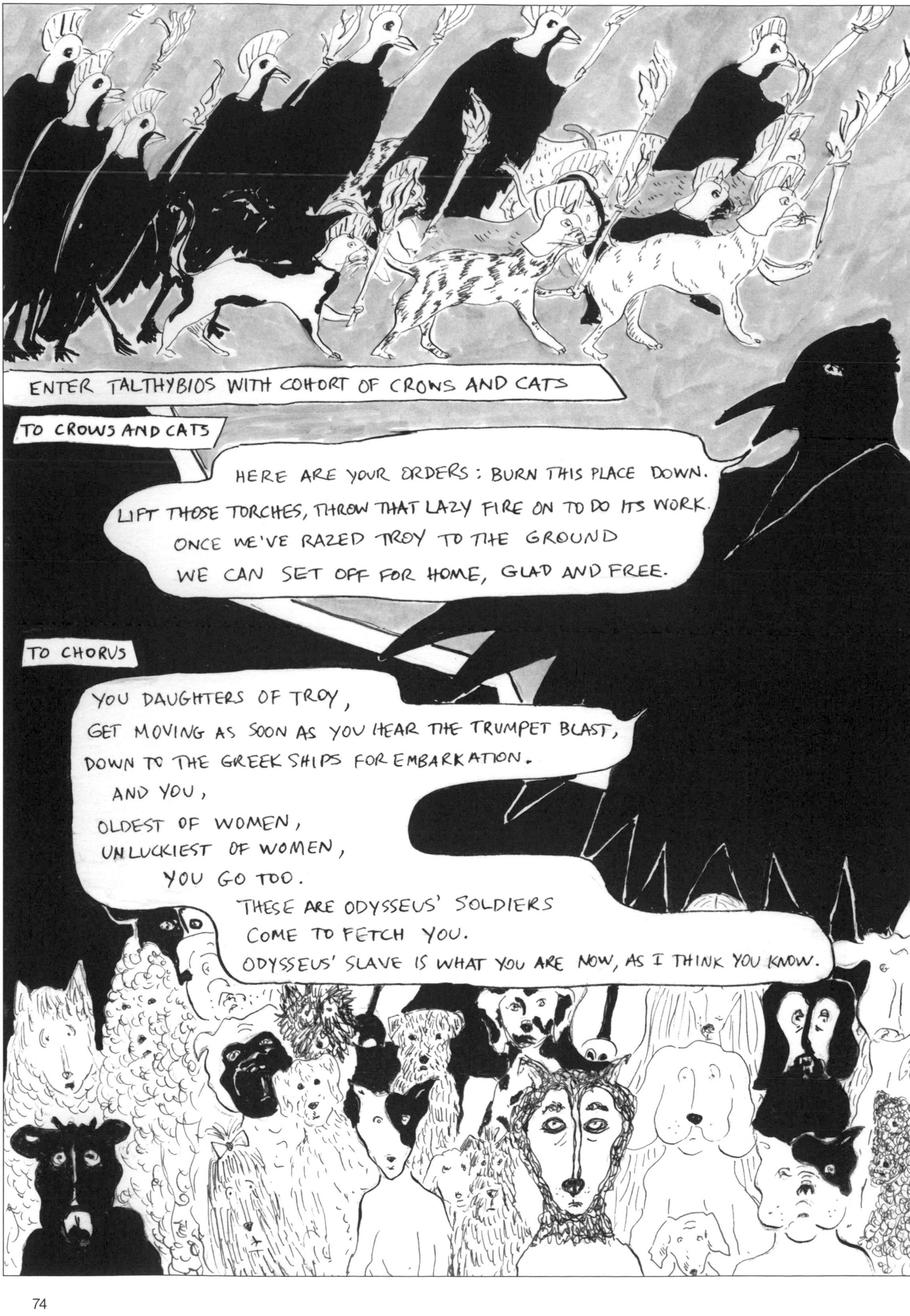
ENTER TALTHYBIOS WITH COHORT OF CROWS AND CATS
TO CROWS AND CATS
HERE ARE YOUR ORDERS: BURN THIS PLACE DOWN. LIFT THOSE TORCHES, THROW THAT LAZY FIRE ON TO DO ITS WORK. ONCE WE'VE RAZED TROY TO THE GROUND WE CAN SET OFF FOR HOME, GLAD AND FREE.
TO CHORUS
YOU DAUGHTERS OF TROY, GET MOVING AS SOON AS YOU HEAR THE TRUMPET BLAST, DOWN TO THE GREEK SHIPS FOR EMBARKATION. AND YOU, OLDEST OF WOMEN, UNLUCKIEST OF WOMEN, YOU GO TOO. THESE ARE ODYSSEUS' SOLDIERS COME TO FETCH YOU. ODYSSEUS' SLAVE IS WHAT YOU ARE NOW, AS I THINK YOU KNOW.

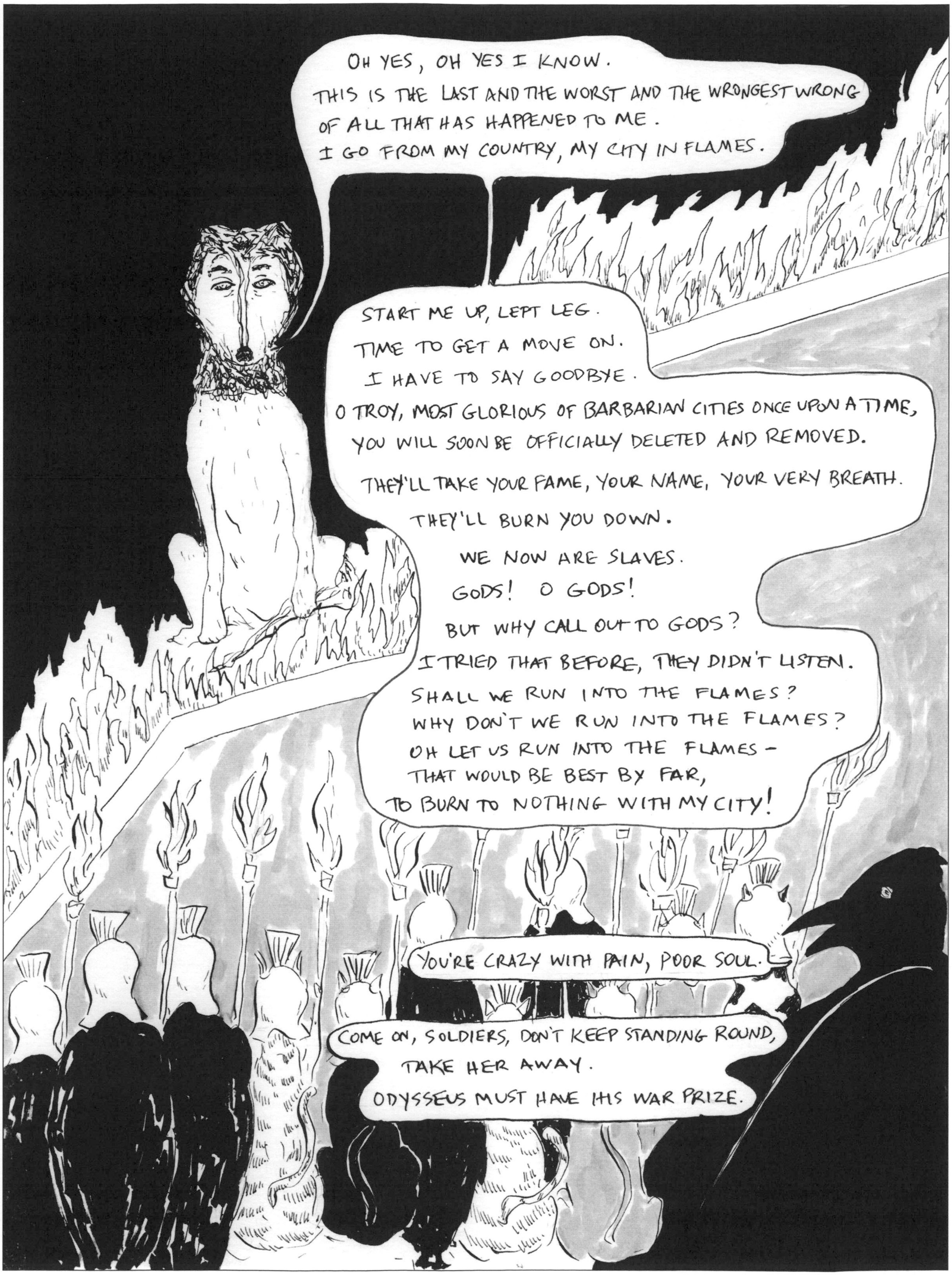

OH YES, OH YES I KNOW.
THIS IS THE LAST AND THE WORST AND THE WRONGEST WRONG
OF ALL THAT HAS HAPPENED TO ME.
I GO FROM MY COUNTRY, MY CITY IN FLAMES.
START ME UP, LEPT LEG.
TIME TO GET A MOVE ON.
I HAVE TO SAY GOODBYE.
O TROY, MOST GLORIOUS OF BARBARIAN CITIES ONCE UPON A TIME,
YOU WILL SOON BE OFFICIALLY DELETED AND REMOVED.
THEY'LL TAKE YOUR FAME, YOUR NAME, YOUR VERY BREATH.
THEY'LL BURN YOU DOWN.
WE NOW ARE SLAVES.
GODS! O GODS!
BUT WHY CALL OUT TO GODS?
I TRIED THAT BEFORE, THEY DIDN'T LISTEN.
SHALL WE RUN INTO THE FLAMES?
WHY DON'T WE RUN INTO THE FLAMES?
OH LET US RUN INTO THE FLAMES -
THAT WOULD BE BEST BY FAR,
TO BURN TO NOTHING WITH MY CITY!
YOU'RE CRAZY WITH PAIN, POOR SOUL.
COME ON, SOLDIERS, DON'T KEEP STANDING ROUND,
TAKE HER AWAY.
ODYSSEUS MUST HAVE HIS WAR PRIZE.

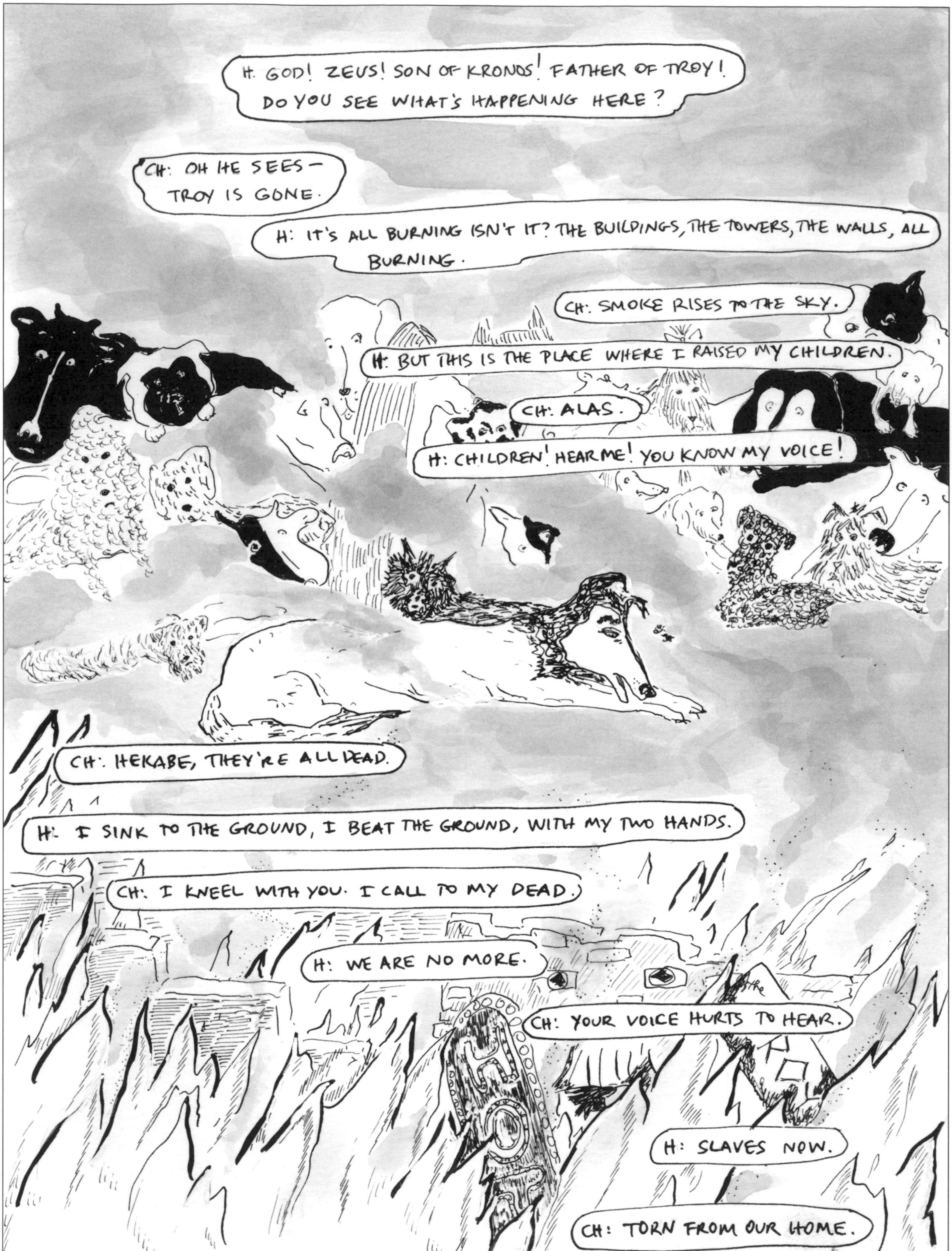
H. GOD! ZEUS! SON OF KRONOS! FATHER OF TROY! DO YOU SEE WHAT'S HAPPENING HERE?
CH: OH HE SEES— TROY IS GONE.
H: IT'S ALL BURNING ISN'T IT? THE BUILDINGS, THE TOWERS, THE WALLS, ALL BURNING.
CH: SMOKE RISES TO THE SKY.
H: BUT THIS IS THE PLACE WHERE I RAISED MY CHILDREN.
CH: ALAS.
H: CHILDREN! HEAR ME! YOU KNOW MY VOICE!
CH: HEKABE, THEY'RE ALL DEAD.
H: I SINK TO THE GROUND, I BEAT THE GROUND, WITH MY TWO HANDS.
CH: I KNEEL WITH YOU. I CALL TO MY DEAD.
H: WE ARE NO MORE.
CH: YOUR VOICE HURTS TO HEAR.
H: SLAVES NOW.
CH: TORN FROM OUR HOME.

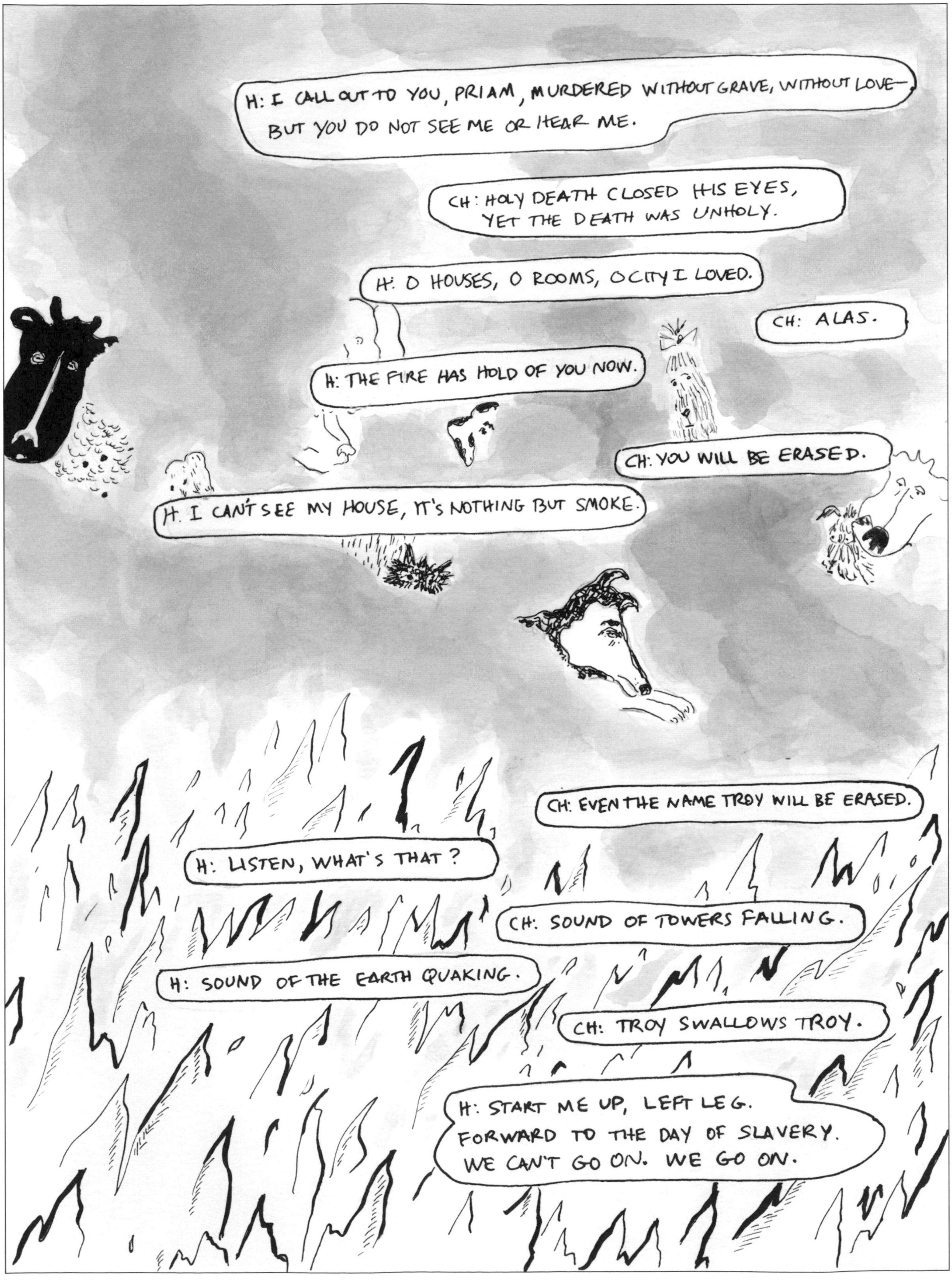
H: I CALL OUT TO YOU, PRIAM, MURDERED WITHOUT GRAVE, WITHOUT LOVE— BUT YOU DO NOT SEE ME OR HEAR ME.
CH: HOLY DEATH CLOSED HIS EYES, YET THE DEATH WAS UNHOLY.
H: O HOUSES, O ROOMS, O CITY I LOVED.
CH: ALAS.
H: THE FIRE HAS HOLD OF YOU NOW.
CH: YOU WILL BE ERASED.
H. I CAN'T SEE MY HOUSE, IT'S NOTHING BUT SMOKE.
CH: EVEN THE NAME TROY WILL BE ERASED.
H: LISTEN, WHAT'S THAT?
CH: SOUND OF TOWERS FALLING.
H: SOUND OF THE EARTH QUAKING.
CH: TROY SWALLOWS TROY.
H: START ME UP, LEFT LEG. FORWARD TO THE DAY OF SLAVERY. WE CAN'T GO ON. WE GO ON.

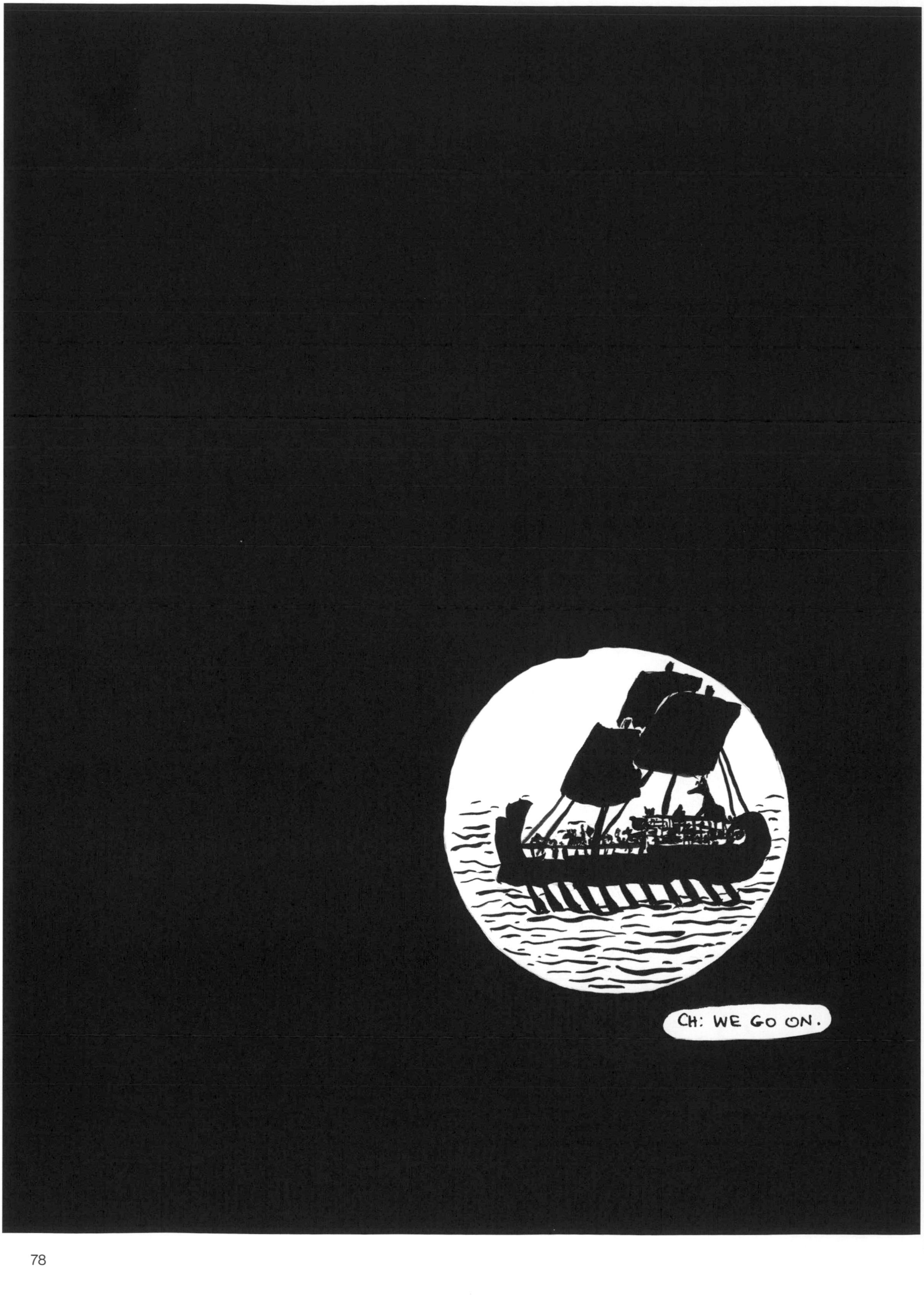
CH: WE GO ON.

Printed in Canada
First published as a New Directions Book in 2021

Library of Congress Cataloging-in-Publication Date
Names: Euripides, author. | Carson, Anne, 1950– translator. | Bruno, Rosanna, illustrator.
Title: The Trojan women : a comic / Euripides ; by Rosanna Bruno ; text by Anne Carson.
Other titles: Trojan women. English (Carson)
Description: First edition. | New York : New Directions Publishing, 2021.
Identifiers: LCCN 2020054946 | ISBN 9780811230797 (cloth)
Subjects: LCSH: Hecuba, Queen of Troy – Comic books, strips, etc. |
Andromache (Legendary character) – Comic books, strips, etc. |
Cassandra (Legendary character) – Comic books, strips, etc. |
Women – Turkey – Troy (Extinct city) – Comic books, strips, etc. |
Women and war – Turkey – Troy (Extinct city) – Comic books, strips, etc. |
War and society – Turkey – Troy (Extinct city) – Comic books, strips, etc. |
LCGFT: Comics (Graphic works) | Graphic novels. | Tragedies (Drama)
Classification: LCC PA3975.T8 C37 2021 | DDC 882/.01 – dc23
LC record available at https://lccn.loc.gov/2020054946

10 9 8 7 6 5 4 3 2 1

New Directions Books are published for James Laughlin
by New Directions Publishing Corporation
80 Eighth Avenue, New York 10011